DEAD PET

DEAD PET

Send Your Best Little Buddy Off in Style

**ANDREW KIRK
& JANE MOSELEY**

The Lyons Press
Guilford, Connecticut
An imprint of The Globe Pequot Press

To buy books in quantity for corporate use
or incentives, call **(800) 962–0973**
or e-mail **premiums@GlobePequot.com**.

Copyright © 2009 by The Ivy Press

First Lyons Press edition, 2009

ALL RIGHTS RESERVED. No part of this book may be reproduced or transmitted in any form by any means, electronic or mechanical, including photocopying and recording, or by any information storage and retrieval system, except as may be expressly permitted in writing from the publisher. Requests for permission should be addressed to The Globe Pequot Press, Attn: Rights and Permissions Department, P.O. Box 480, Guilford, CT 06437.

The Lyons Press is an imprint of The Globe Pequot Press.

Library of Congress Cataloging-in-Publication Data is available on file.

ISBN 978-1-59921-570-9

Printed in China

10 9 8 7 6 5 4 3 2 1

This book was conceived, designed, and produced by:
Ivy Press
210 High Street,
Lewes, East Sussex, BN7 2NS, UK.

Creative Director Peter Bridgewater
Publisher Jason Hook
Editorial Director Tom Kitch
Senior Project Editor Polita Caaveiro
Art Director Wayne Blades
Designer Ginny Zeal
Illustrator Ivan Hissey

To the full extent permissible by law, the authors and publishers shall have no liability for any loss or damage to a pet (dead, decomposing, alive, or just plain unwell), however it arises, resulting from anyone who does not comprehend that this is a work of humor. If you are a pet lover, animal rights activist, or simply lack the necessary funny bone to follow along, you are advised to immediately watch ten consecutive screenings of *Lassie Come Home*; read Evelyn Waugh's book *The Loved One*; and undergo a ten-week dog training course with Paris Hilton. And… please don't shoot your beloved pet off into space until you are sure he's really, really dead.

CONTENTS

- 6 Introduction

PREPARING FOR THE END
- 10 Before They Go
- 12 Insurance
- 14 Cloning Your Pet
- 16 Choosing a Grave Location
- 18 The Final Hours—Saying Goodbye
- 20 Sudden Death

IMMEDIATE ACTION
- 24 How to Be Sure it's the End
- 26 Telling the Family
- 28 Preservation
- 30 Embalming
- 32 Cryogenic Eternity
- 34 Taxidermy
- 36 Excarnation

CHOICE OF COFFIN
- 40 Coffins: Some General Principles
- 44 Coffins for Insects, Large and Small
- 48 Coffins for Reptiles
- 52 Coffins for Small Rodents
- 54 Coffins for Rabbits and Large Rodents
- 56 Coffins for Fish
- 60 Coffins for Cats
- 64 Coffins for Dogs
- 68 Finishing and Lining the Coffin

THE FUNERAL
- 74 Vigils and Wakes
- 76 Floral Tributes
- 78 Hearses
- 80 The Funeral Procession
- 82 Order of Service
- 84 Eulogies and Readings
- 86 Pagan Rites
- 88 Humanist Funerals
- 90 Personalizing the Rites
- 94 Holding a Reception

THE INTERMENT
- 98 Family Graves
- 100 Cremation
- 102 Sea Burial
- 104 Sky Burial
- 106 Grave Goods
- 108 Headstones
- 110 Urns and Mausoleums

THE AFTERMATH
- 114 The Mourning Period
- 116 Memorial Services
- 118 Seances
- 120 Internet Memorials
- 122 Your Pet's Worldly Goods
- 124 Moving on

- 126 Glossary
- 127 Further Reading and Useful Web sites
- 128 Index

INTRODUCTION

The death of a beloved companion can be a devastating experience. The close bond that develops over many years is such that no one else can really understand the pain you are going through—a lifetime of shared habits, interests, outlooks, and opinions suddenly and irretrievably taken from you. And when the companion in question is an animal, the loss may feel somehow worse. This creature depended on you for everything, and reflected those aspects of your personality that you considered most attractive. Alert to your moods, soothing the daily stresses and frustrations of your workaday existence, always delighted to see you, and never tiring of the sound of your voice—little wonder such a bereavement can seem unendurable.

Planning and organizing a sensitive and appropriate funeral for your pet is one small way of assuaging the inner hurt and sending the animal gently into that good night. This book will guide you through this most difficult life experience, from the moment that you realize your friend has gone forever, through

INTRODUCTION

the details of coffins and orders of service, to the committal and the reception afterward. It considers practical, emotional, and spiritual issues, and caters to all types of pets and a wide range of possible responses to the question of what to do when they have gone. Written with sensitivity and understanding—but without shying away from the essential matters that need to be faced—this book explains how to orchestrate, with a little thought and effort, a fine memorial to show everyone just how much your relationship with your pet meant to you.

His friends he loved.
His fellest earthly foes—
Cats—I believe he did but feign to hate.
My hand will miss the insinuated nose,
Mine eyes that tail that wagged contempt at Fate.

Sir William Watson, "*Epitaph on a Dog*"

PREPARING FOR THE END

PREPARING FOR THE END

BEFORE THEY GO

Fig. 1. **If your pet refuses to sit still for its portrait, you could ask the veterinarian for a very low dose of tranquilizer to help it relax into its pose.**

It's no good wishing that you'd kept a record of your pet's special qualities after it has actually passed on. Plan ahead, and prepare really meaningful mementoes that will act as a comfort in later years. If you're an art lover, consider getting a professional portrait done. Portraitists are most familiar with cats and dogs as subjects, but a really good artist should be able to catch the true spirit of your loved one—even if your pet is an iguana or a mouse. Introduce the artist to your pet to make sure there is a rapport. Remember to ask the artist to capture a characteristic pose, and take a few photographs to help him or her if you own something restless such as a tarantula or a gerbil.

Fig. 2. **Nothing helps you to remember your pet better than the sound of its voice. Get your dog to bark, your parrot to shriek, or your cat to meow into a microphone. Even the rhythmic noise of a hamster running on its wheel can be strongly evocative. You could use that special sound as the ring tone on your cell phone, to serve as an eternal reminder of your relationship.**

BEFORE THEY GO

If your budget doesn't allow for professional art, use your own photographs, choosing only the best likenesses. Once you've selected an image, modern technology means that you don't have to stick to photo albums and framed pictures—you'll be able to scan and use your favorite image on any number of household items, from mouse pads to pillows. Get a familiar pose printed onto a T-shirt so that you can literally wear your loved one next to your heart; or commission one of the many specialist fabric-printing companies to make a repeat print of the picture, so that you can create themed upholstery or drapes.

Fig. 3. You can make your workspace a little shrine to memories—provided you've equipped yourself with the raw material before your pet passes on.

PREPARING FOR THE END

INSURANCE

No one would dream of suggesting that you can put a value on your pet's life, but while it may seem indelicate to raise the matter, there is no escaping the fact that illness and death cost money. So it is wise to make the necessary financial arrangements before the time comes to start signing checks. When buying insurance, you should take care to consider various factors. Is your pet of a species that is prone to particular chronic illnesses, such as hip dysplasia or arthritis? Does your pet have the kind of outgoing and risk-taking personality that is liable to lead to accidents involving moving vehicles, large dogs, deep water, or tall buildings? Are your funeral plans situated at the unvarnished or the extravagant end of the spectrum?

> *But when we are certain of sorrow in store,*
> *Why do we always arrange for more?*
> *Brothers and Sisters, I bid you beware*
> *Of giving your heart to a dog to tear.*
>
> Rudyard Kipling, *"The Power of the Dog"*

INSURANCE

Fig. 1. Time spent preparing for
the final moment is never wasted.
It can also save money in the end.

These issues should be considered before you choose an insurance plan. You will want to check how easy it is to make a claim, and whether there is a veterinary helpline and bereavement counseling service. You will also want to check whether the policy covers death by flood or fire or lightning strike. Of course none of these thoughts are pleasant, but it is best to face the worst and make provision for it. Once the policy is chosen and the payments start going out, you can file the documents away safely and get on with enjoying your pet's companionship.

PREPARING FOR THE END

CLONING YOUR PET

Cloning is a truly innovative way to ensure that your pet stays with you forever. It's rare and expensive, and is currently more viable for some species than for others. But if you really feel that your life will become impossibly bleak and gray without Rex, Sooty, or Nibbles, this is the only sure-fire way to keep your beloved pet present for as long as you need it. Before you invest, though, you need to ask yourself the question: Will you feel the same about Sooty II? Or even Sootys III, IV, V, and VI? If you answer yes, make inquiries.

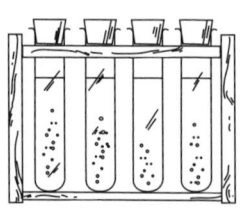

Fig. 1. **Science can be your best friend when you long to preserve your pet forever.**

The cloning of cats and dogs is almost at a commercially viable stage now, but with more unusual pets you may have to wait a while for science to catch up and enable you to be reunited with your friend. In the meantime, the way to make sure you're prepared when the time comes is to pay a professional

... he will be our friend for always and always and always.

Rudyard Kipling

CLONING YOUR PET

laboratory to take a small sample of your pet's cells (nothing invasive—usually just a skin scrape) and cryopreserve them to keep that precious DNA viable. Admittedly, the resulting cloned Sooty will be a surrogate, but what you'll ultimately get is your original pet, reborn. In price terms, the fees will probably be equivalent to buying a top-of-the-line automobile or a beach house. Still, who can value love in investment terms? As the commercials say: Priceless. To recoup some of the funds spent on the cloning itself, you might want to propose your pets are used in an advertizing campaign. Repeat fees could be substantial.

Fig. 2. Why stick at one? Multiple cloning is achievable, and may be cheaper.

PREPARING FOR THE END

CHOOSING A GRAVE LOCATION

Maybe there's a favorite hilltop where you used to sit together side by side; maybe your cat had a particular scratching spot in the garden, which seems a natural place for her to be laid to rest. The best grave locations, though, are those that you can choose jointly while your pet is still with you. Particularly for pets that are usually kept indoors or confined in a cage, an outing to seek out and decide upon a grave spot can be enjoyable.

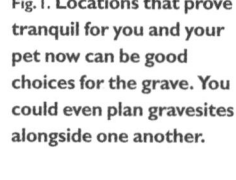

Fig. 1. Locations that prove tranquil for you and your pet now can be good choices for the grave. You could even plan gravesites alongside one another.

CHOOSING A GRAVE LOCATION

Fig. 2. **Try to choose somewhere visually attractive that will be a comfort after the bereavement.**

Pick a mild day (you don't want your gerbil, mouse, or tropical bird to meet an untimely end by catching cold) and visit some local beauty spots—they can be as local as your backyard, or you can travel a little farther afield. Seek out somewhere you will be happy to visit after your bereavement, but be aware of practical considerations. The local authorities may take a dim view of pet graves on public ground, so when choosing a suitable site check out the bylaws, as well as considering your own and your pet's preference. When you think you've found the perfect place, sit there together for a while and share some quality time. Don't hurry over this important decision—if you're planning to come here often in future, you want to be sure you've chosen well.

Fig. 3. **Habits you may find irritating when your pet is still with you—nibbling in your favorite flower garden, say—will be seen much more fondly when they are gone, and may inform your choice of a final resting place.**

PREPARING FOR THE END

THE FINAL HOURS—SAYING GOODBYE

Unless your pet is of a species that has a chance of outliving you (step forward, tortoise owners and parrot fanciers), there will come a moment when the realization dawns that its days (or even hours) are numbered. Perhaps the veterinarian has been called and pronounced his or her verdict on your companion, and you've been informed that to let the situation go on much longer would be unfair to your pet. You've been encouraged to start reflecting on the wonderful times you've shared. When you hear this—it's a common utterance for veterinarians—take a little time. Don't rush things; those last hours are precious. When the moment comes, compose yourself to say goodbye, then ask the veterinarian to bring your pet gently to a peaceful end.

Fig. 1. When you get the unwelcome news, reflect for a few minutes on the special times you've shared and the happiness your pet has brought you.

Fig. 2. At some point it will become clear that your pet should be given help to be taken to a happier place.

Fig. 3. Obtain some chloroform from the veterinarian. Most will also advise on an appropriate dosage, free of charge.

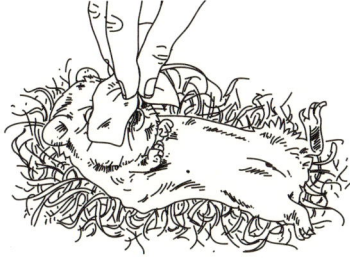

Fig. 4. Moisten a small pad of cotton with the correct amount of the drug. Place it gently over the face of the sick animal. Hold it there for at least five minutes.

Fig. 5. The moment has passed. Remove the cotton pad. You can now start the grieving process.

If you're a strong person and you worry about the ultimate cost, you can perform this latter task yourself on small animals with a little pad soaked in chloroform (*see above*). Larger animals, though, are best left to the professionals. Make sure that your pet, if conscious, does not see or hear you behaving in a distressed fashion. Stay as calm as you can during the final minutes; it will be easier for you both at the moment of parting.

PREPARING FOR THE END

SUDDEN DEATH

Sometimes there's no warning, and no time to prepare. Your parrot falls off her perch, your hamster just doesn't get up (being nocturnal, he's never been all that keen on mornings anyway). You may find yourself surprised by your reaction: at first, you may feel nothing much. Give yourself an hour or two to absorb the situation; don't do anything immediately—although you may not want to leave it too long. Be kind to yourself, and take a little time to get over the shock before you act. You'll find that it is valuable to access your grief once the numbness passes, and it is unhealthy to keep it bottled up and unexpressed, whether your feelings concern a border collie or a stick insect.

Fig. 1. Remember that sudden death always results in a shock, even if you don't feel it at first. Ultimately, it's probably easier on the deceased than on those left behind.

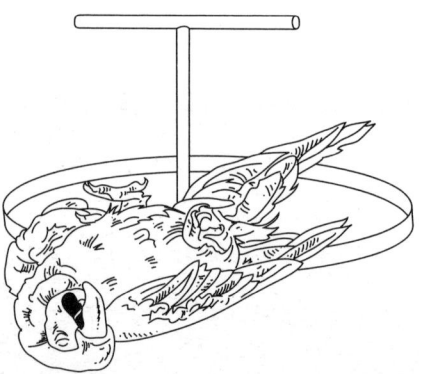

SUDDEN DEATH

Once it begins to sink in, you need to decide what to do next. Smaller pets are almost always buried at home, while it's more usual to leave larger species—from cats and dogs upward—to the veterinarian. There aren't any rules about this, however: it's up to you how you want the mortal remains of your pet dealt with, and what you wish to do yourself (and how). If you haven't ever thought beyond the moment of your pet's passing, sit down and write some notes, drawing up a rough plan for what you feel would be best to happen next. You'll find this (and the following chapters) especially helpful in gathering your thoughts at this emotional time.

Fig. 2. **Never, ever flush even the tiniest pet—not even a goldfish.**

Many birds and beasts are ... as fit to go to Heaven as many human beings—people who talk of their seats there with as much confidence as if they had booked them at a box-office.

Leigh Hunt

IMMEDIATE ACTION

IMMEDIATE ACTION

HOW TO BE SURE IT'S THE END

Remember that you're an amateur in the field of death. If a veterinarian isn't present, be sure to make all the necessary checks before you assume the worst. Hibernation can make it look as though a pet has died, and you wouldn't be the first to cremate the family tortoise in error. And, just like hibernation, a fit or a coma may be reversible.

If an insect or spider is on its back, its legs curled inward, it is deceased (a very few species of large spider are able to feign death, but they are unlikely to be kept as pets). Similarly, a bird lying inert, legs pointed skyward, can generally be safely assumed to be dead. Finally, if a fish is floating belly-up in its tank, it has probably passed away.

Fig. 1. **It's far more straightforward to tell whether some species are dead than others.**

HOW TO BE SURE IT'S THE END

Take your pet's pulse (it's easier at the neck than at the paw) and use a pocket mirror to see if he is breathing (*see right*). Rigor mortis usually sets in after about three hours, but this is much more obvious in a furry mammal than, say, a scaly reptile. A motionless python, for example, might simply be resting after an unusually large lunch.

Fig. 2. **Take a small pocket mirror and hold it just in front of your pet's mouth and nose. Watch to see if a faint mist forms. If it does—even if you can't see the chest rising and falling—your pet is breathing.**

Fig. 3. **Even if the mirror doesn't mist over, you need to make doubly sure. Gently lay your pet on its side in the classic recovery position. Wait for three hours.**

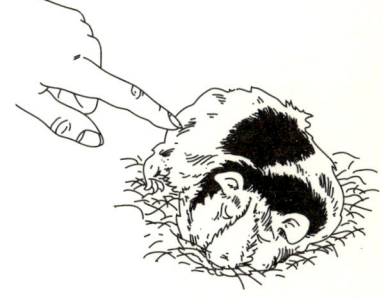

Fig. 4. **If there is no sign of life after the allotted period of time, and your pet is beginning to feel stiff and "set" when poked lightly with your forefinger, it is probably safe to presume that he is dead.**

IMMEDIATE ACTION

TELLING THE FAMILY

If you were the one who discovered the departed, it is your unenviable duty to tell the rest of the family. (Single pet owners will not have to face this; conversely, it may mean that there is no one with whom you can freely share the intensity of your grief.) If the people to whom you have to break your sad news are young children, there are two ways to handle things: you can bite the bullet and offer the facts straight, without embellishment; or you can break them down into stages (the classic ones are "unwell," "rather worse," and "at peace now") to defer the shock. Time breaking the news carefully; just before school is probably not a good idea.

Fig. 1. **Bereaved family members cannot always cope with seeing their loved one in death but if they are strong enough, saying goodbye may help them to move on, after a suitable period of grieving.**

Even more delicacy is required if the deceased pet in question belonged to the children—especially if it was not greatly loved by you. Remember that even if you didn't much care for the hamster or the goldfish, a child's first experience of death requires sensitive handling. If your children already have a belief system (religious or rationalist), do be sure that your explanation fits in with it, in order to avoid confusion. It doesn't matter whether they believe that Sheba has gone to heaven to be with Jesus now, or whether they accept that Sheba now lives for them only in happy memories and fond thoughts, provided that whichever explanation you give will also hold water for Grandma, when her time comes. Children often demand answers to the big questions and it is good to prepared with your own considered and appropriate response. Remember: Death is a part of the great mystery of life, and everyone is going to experience it at least once.

> *Lord, look down on Thy Servant!*
> *Bad things have come to pass.*
> *There is no heat in the midday sun,*
> *nor health in the wayside grass.*
> *His bones are full of an old disease—*
> *his torments run and increase.*
> *Lord, make haste with Thy Lightnings*
> *and grant him a quick release!*
>
> Rudyard Kipling, *"His Apologies"*

IMMEDIATE ACTION

PRESERVATION

While you will obviously be distracted in the immediate aftermath of bereavement, it is important to remember some practical details. Timing is all. If you have decided to deal with the arrangements yourself for committing your pet to whatever the afterlife may hold, you will need to move relatively quickly. Rigor mortis will usually begin to set in about three hours after death, and though it will wear off again a couple of days later, it may make it very difficult for you to store your pet in the days leading up to the funeral if all his legs are sticking straight out at odd angles. This would also be a most undignified way for your companion to spend his final days in your household.

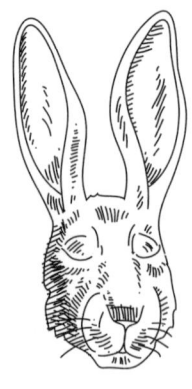

Fig. 1. You want your pet to look his best, so take some care to lay out the body.

You should first arrange the body of the deceased in a restful pose, or alternatively in a compact posture if you are not going to be able to attend to the funeral for some time and need to store the remains. Tuck the legs in and don't forget about the tail and any long ears. Then seal the body of the deceased in an airtight container such as a stout plastic bag and put

Fig. 2. Legs and ears should be arranged before rigor mortis sets in.

PRESERVATION

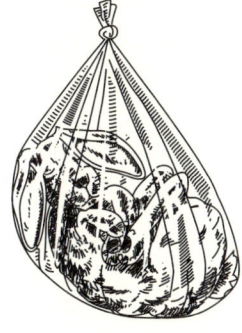

Fig. 3. **Put the body of the deceased in a clear bag to avoid misidentification.**

Fig. 4. **If you have to put the deceased in the freezer make sure the body is clearly labeled.**

it in the refrigerator, or at least a cold cellar. The deceased will keep like this for a couple of days, but if there is going to be a longer period of mourning before the committal you should embalm the body as described on the following pages.

You will need to ensure there is no danger of vermin or predators—or even your remaining pets—interfering with the deceased in whatever location the remains are stored. There is no need to freeze the body unless you are about to go away and won't have time to organize the funeral before you leave. If you do decide to freeze your pet's corpse, make sure that your housemates know it is in the freezer, and label the package clearly, otherwise it might not be there when you get back.

> *She did not know that she was dead,*
> *But when the pang was o'er,*
> *Sat down to wait her Master's tread*
> *Upon the Golden Floor.*
>
> Rudyard Kipling, *"Dinah in Heaven"*

EMBALMING

Fig. 1. Place the body of the deceased in a relaxed pose.

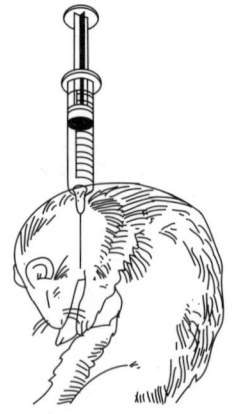

Fig. 2. Inject the embalming fluid into the carotid artery.

After death, physical decomposition begins immediately, so if there is likely to be a delay between your pet's passing over and the performance of the appropriate rites, or if you enjoy a particularly warm climate, you will want to take steps to stop this process of decay. While freezing will slow the process, it does not allow for a dignified period of lying in state, and a better approach is to embalm the body. This involves draining the bodily fluids and replacing them with a preservative. Formaldehyde performs this function particularly effectively.

You should first set the body, by placing it into a relaxed and lifelike pose, which the embalming chemicals will preserve. The eyeballs will depress into the eye sockets, so you should put a small wad of cotton between the eyes and the eyelids to plump them out; you should also seal the mouth shut by sewing the lower jaw to the upper, inside the mouth so that the stitches don't show. When

EMBALMING

the corpse is tastefully arranged, you need to recall from high school lessons how blood circulates the living body and apply the same process: the embalming fluid is pumped into the cardiovascular system via the carotid artery, while the blood is drained from a pipe inserted in a vein. This is the all-important process by which the preservative fluid penetrates all the body tissues. The internal organs should be punctured via an incision in the abdomen and the contents pumped out, before a further preservative solution is injected into the cavities.

Fig. 3. **While the embalming fluid goes in, blood can be drained into a receptacle.**

Finally, you may wish to apply some moisturizer to the lips and nostrils, which are likely to dry out, and some blush if you are attending to a rodent that would ordinarily have had ruddy cheeks. You will now have given your pet a beautiful corpse to carry forward to the ceremony. Capture your skills for future reference on film.

Fig. 4. **You could copy the ancient Egyptians and remove the internal organs for separate storage, but this is not obligatory.**

CRYOGENIC ETERNITY

No longer reserved solely for eccentric billionaires, cryogenic preservation is now a service that is offered for pets, too. After all, the cure for Fluffy's final illness may be only a few years away. And a great side benefit of a cryogenic disposal is that it keeps even the smallest glimmers of hope alive.

Cryogenic preservation is, essentially, a very deep deep-freeze. The intention is to preserve your pet until science has advanced to the point at which whatever health breakdown or accident caused its demise can be reversed. Of course, you are traveling hopefully—but, looking at the immense advances in science that have occurred over just the last decade or two, there is every expectation that the happy day of your reunion with your pet may arrive within your own lifetime.

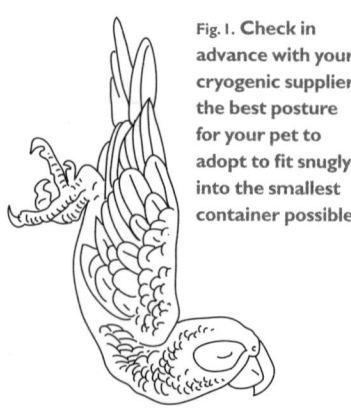

Fig. 1. **Check in advance with your cryogenic supplier the best posture for your pet to adopt to fit snugly into the smallest container possible.**

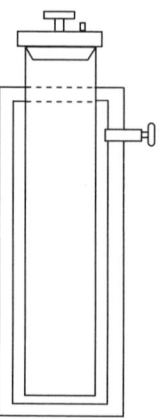

Fig. 2. **The specialist will be in charge of putting your pet into the cryogenic container.**

CRYOGENIC ETERNITY

You will need to locate a cryogenic specialist, and the costs may be quite considerable. On the plus side, there will be no side expenses; the container in which your pet will go into the freezer will be supplied as part of the service. You should, though, be aware that the overall expenditure will be affected by the cubic space that your companion occupies, so don't be tempted into opting for a container larger than necessary for your loved one (*see page 32, Fig. 1*). If you want to organize a funeral, this can probably be arranged, cylinder-side, through your cryogenic supplier, although enthusiasts will tell you that there's no need for the usual farewells: think of it as a relationship on hold, or on ice, but not at an end. Absence may indeed make the heart, if not the body, grow fonder. With cryogenics, it's only ever "*à bientôt*."

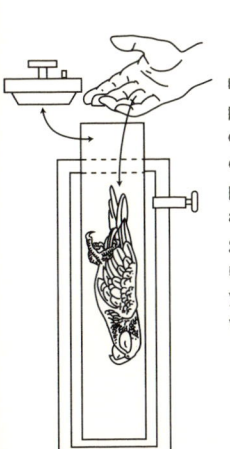

Fig. 3. **Once your pet is comfortably ensconced, the container will be put into storage, and you will be given the necessary references so that you can recall it when you need to.**

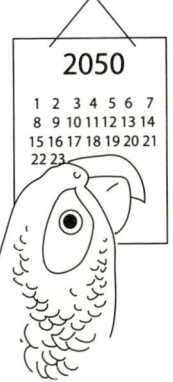

Fig. 4. **When the arrangements have been completed, all you need to do is conjure up a happy image of the day of your future reunion.**

IMMEDIATE ACTION

TAXIDERMY

If you really cannot bear the idea of not having your pet around any more, there is one method of retaining his presence in body, if not in spirit. Taxidermy is the process of preserving the hide of an animal on a mold that gives it a lifelike appearance. Professional taxidermists are increasingly offering this service to bereaved pet owners who are unable to say goodbye, and a relatively small fee will give you the chance to keep your pet in perpetuity.

Fig. 1. **Make an incision along the length of the skin without piercing the body.**

It is perfectly possible to perform this rite yourself, particularly if the companion in question is fairly small. After all, since during its lifetime your pet was reliant on you to perform any number of considerate tasks, how appropriate it seems to share one last intimate ritual. Think of it as the last kind act you can perform for your pet on earth.

> *Animals have these advantages over man:*
> *They have no theologians to instruct them,*
> *their funerals cost them nothing, and no*
> *one starts lawsuits over their wills.*
>
> Voltaire

TAXIDERMY

Fig. 2. **Spread out the removed skin and treat it with preservative.**

There are three steps in the process of taxidermy: skinning, preserving, and mounting. Skinning is relatively easy if you have a sharp knife and a steady hand, and is much like peeling off a sock. The head is the trickiest part, because you need to ensure that the ears remain attached and that you cut carefully around the eyes. Once the skin is removed, it can be treated with borax, which kills any bacteria and preserves the skin in good condition. Slip the skin over an appropriately shaped mold, sew up the main incision, then add the glass eyes, and it will be as if your pet had never gone away. Constant companionship can bring great solace.

Fig. 3. **Place the skin over the mold and stitch it up neatly.**

IMMEDIATE ACTION

EXCARNATION

Fig. 1. **If you are of an environmentally minded disposition and accustomed to living in harmony with the planet, the ritual of excarnation—Nature's way— might be of real comfort to you.**

Excarnation is an ancient death ritual known to have been practiced in the European Iron Age. It is also associated with certain Native American tribes and with Tibetan Buddhism. The dead body is left in the open so that the soft tissues are stripped away by predators and the elements, leaving only the skeleton behind. In our modern, sanitized culture, this is likely to arouse feelings of revulsion in some readers, but consider for a moment the ecological implications. Ashes to ashes, dust to dust —what could be more natural than to let Nature take its course? This eco-friendly solution might become increasingly popular in times to come.

You should prepare an altar of some kind: either a large flat stone or a piece of wood. Unless you live in the wilderness, you may need to travel some distance to find a suitably tranquil spot in which to leave your companion. After a few days you can return to collect the remaining bones, which you can then keep in a casket or even mount in an artistic or anatomically correct disposition. This ecologically responsible ritual uses no fuel, no land, and no materials other than those that Nature provides. It offers sustenance for the animals of the wild and enables your pet to fulfill the process of Nature, completing the cosmic cycle of birth and life and death and return.

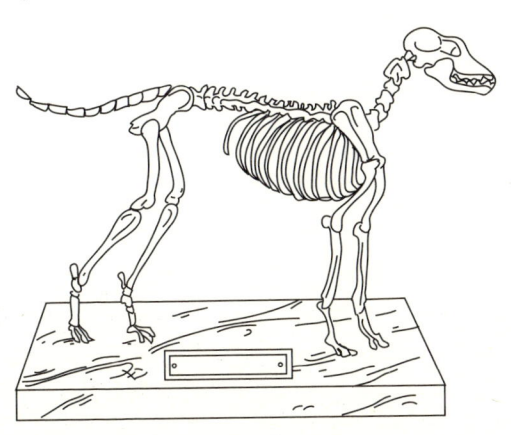

Fig. 2. **If you have scientific interests you could mount the cleaned skeleton as an educational memorial.**

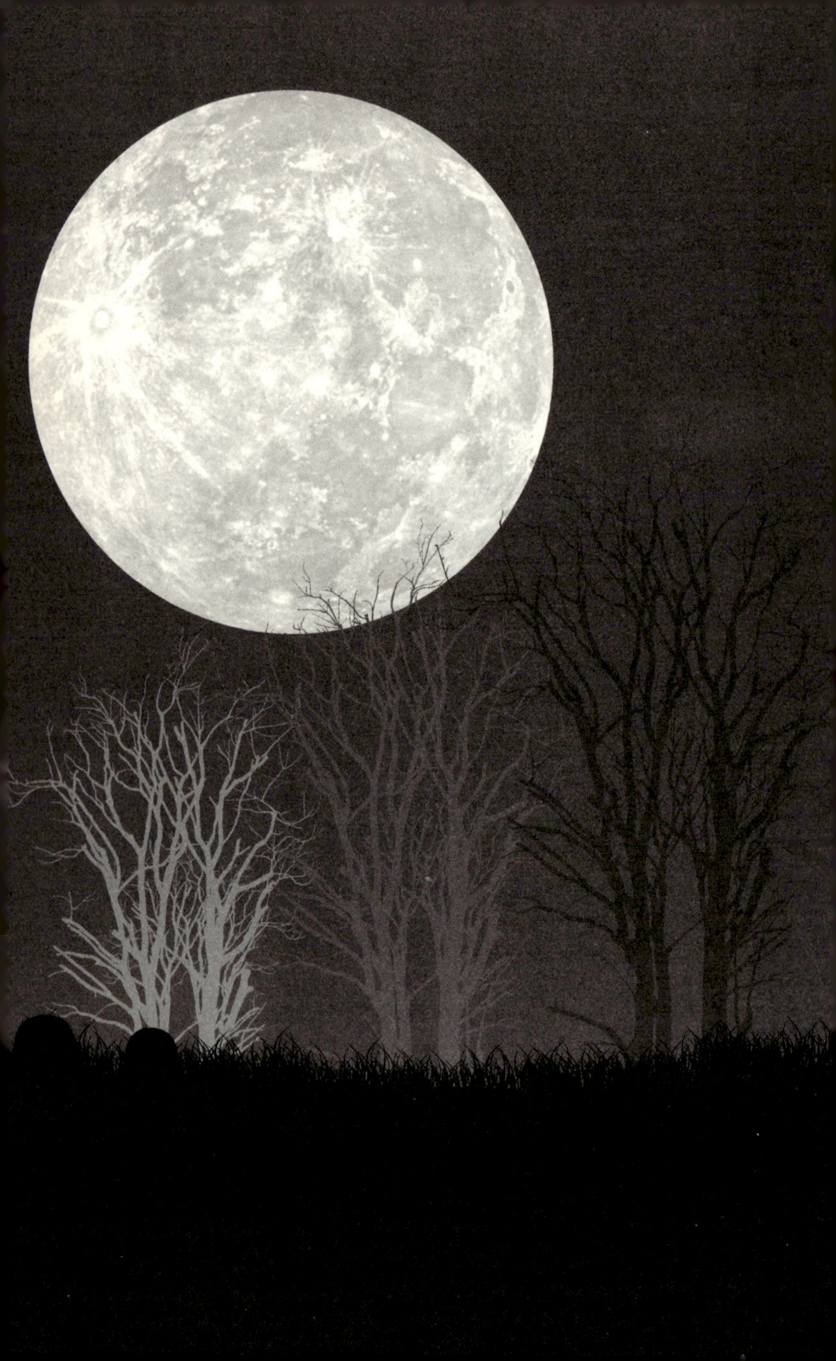

CHOICE OF COFFIN

CHOICE OF COFFIN

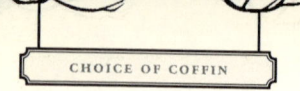

COFFINS: SOME GENERAL PRINCIPLES

A coffin or casket performs two important funereal functions. It protects and carries the body of the deceased on the way to its final resting place, but it also provides a final opportunity for those left behind to show their love and respect for the deceased, through the decoration and quality of the casket itself. The choice of materials and degree of ornamentation can either take the form of a display of ostentation, or a more considered reflection on the character and personality of the coffin's occupier.

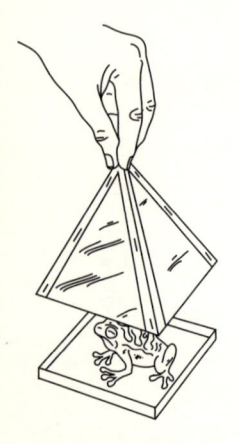

Fig 1. **Coffins can be made to any shape or size.**

Since it will take center stage at the funeral service, the choice of coffin needs to be made with considered care, and you should think about the kind of effect you wish to create: affectionate without being overly sentimental; highly wrought, but not vulgar; simple, but not—how shall we put it?—cheap. It is of course possible to choose a coffin from a proprietary range, but in keeping with the overall feel of this book, we have assumed that you would wish to follow a more personal route. In this section we therefore offer a range of ideas for custom-made caskets to suit all

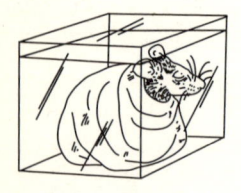

Fig 2. **A clear glass or acrylic coffin allows the deceased to be displayed for visitors to pay their respects.**

GENERAL PRINCIPLES

kinds of pets, some of which can perfectly easily be made by the bereaved themselves as a tangible sign of enduring affection.

There are a number of considerations. The coffin should be a suitable fit for your pet, whatever his size or shape. The materials used should be biodegradable, but sufficiently sturdy to support the weight of the deceased. If you intend to observe a period of lying-in, then a lid that opens or a transparent panel should be part of the design. Ensure that the lid opens smoothly and with ease in order to avoid unwanted awkwardness or interruption at a time of intense emotion. Finally, there is the question of external appearance.

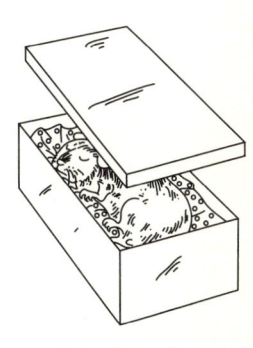

Fig 3. A simple cardboard box might be all you need to send your pet into the hereafter.

Fig 4. A wooden coffin can be ordered from a cabinet maker in just the same way as a human coffin.

There is nothing sweeter than his peace when at rest, for there is nothing brisker than his life when in motion.

Christopher Smart, *"For I will consider my Cat Jeoffrey"*

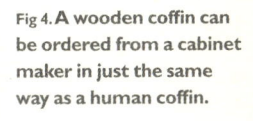

CHOICE OF COFFIN

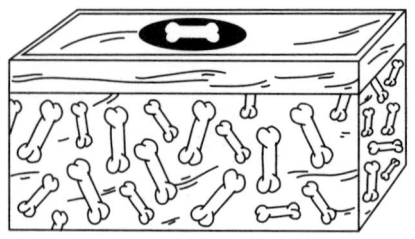

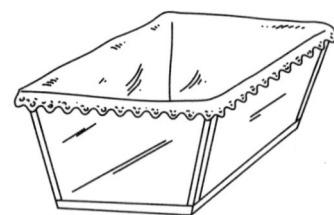

Fig 1.

Fig 2.

Fig 1. You should match the coffin decoration to the species and the personality of your former pet.

Fig 2. A feminine touch is easily added with the use of some lace or embroidery.

When thinking about the external decoration of the coffin, you need to be clear about the kind of impression that you are trying to make on the assembled mourners. Remember that for some of them this will be the first time that the reality of the situation becomes apparent, and you will not want this moment to be marred by an injudicious choice of ornamentation.

Think about your pet's personality. Was he loud and boisterous, in which case bright colors might be appropriate? Or more dignified and reserved, suggesting a somber decorative scheme? Was your pet accustomed to the finer things of life, so that nothing less than solid oak, gold metalwork, and perhaps a catafalque with embroidered draperies

GENERAL PRINCIPLES

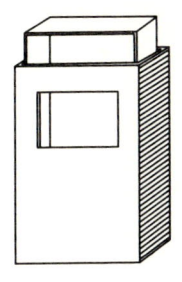

Fig 3.

Fig 4.

would be acceptable? Then again perhaps he was of a more homely disposition, so that a plain box with simply the name of the departed inscribed on the lid would be most fitting.

There is no correct response to this issue—you are the person best placed to decide what your pet would have wanted. Do not, under any circumstances, leave the matter to someone else. Just as with human funerals, these can be occasions when several voices contend to offer their own version of the deceased, and you need to assume charge of the situation. Since you were the individual instrumental in establishing and maintaining your pet's living quarters, it is best that you perform the same service with regard to his deathly resting place.

Fig 3. A painted matchbox with a viewing panel cut into it makes a neat coffin.

Fig 4. For a really green send-off you could weave a coffin from twigs or reeds.

CHOICE OF COFFIN

COFFINS FOR INSECTS, LARGE AND SMALL

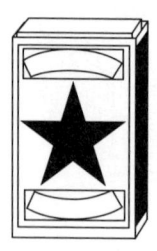

Fig 1. A simple matchbox fulfils the dual role of final vessel and display cabinet for small or not yet fully-fledged insects gone to their maker.

Custom-made coffins don't usually come as small as the size of your insect pet may demand, so you will probably be forced to innovate. A matchbox may be an obvious container, but every type of small box can come into play. Jewelry boxes are particularly appropriate here: what pet could complain about going to his final rest in an elegant pale-blue Tiffany coffin? The single units of egg cartons are perfect for smaller pets (creative owners can glue two together and ornament the result to emulate the grandeur of a Fabergé egg), while, in Pharaoh-fashion, a jelly jar full of his favorite food and respectfully labeled may be appropriate for a stick insect. Use your knowledge of international or historical customs, or in the absence of such, your imagination.

Fig. 2. The ancient Egyptians always provided plenty of food for the departed in the afterlife. Consider doing the same for your insect friend.

COFFINS FOR INSECTS

Because insects are generally among the tinier pets, it's good to enhance their containers to make it clear that, small though they may have been, they occupied a place in your heart out of all proportion to their size. Even if you're going for a utilitarian coffin, consider ornamenting it richly—after all, it's much easier and quicker to do this for a beetle, say, than for a golden retriever. Craft stores sell flat-backed cabochon "jewels" that will flash and glitter to splendid effect, if adhered densely all over even a humble matchbox. Touches of tasteful bling can be appropriate for species who enjoyed flashes of Nature's glamor in life. Use your discretion.

Fig. 3. An unadorned casket with a transparent lid will allow you to gaze on winged beauties in death just as in life.

> But I'll take that vacant spot of floor
> and empty muted hall
> and lay them with the absent voice
> and unused dish along the wall.
>
> I'll wrap these treasured memorials
> in a blanket of my love
> and keep them for my best friend
> until we meet above.
>
> Anonymous

CHOICE OF COFFIN

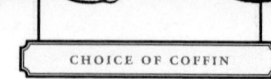

Although the word "coffin" implies a container for interment, many insects are both portable and ornamental, so it's worth considering keeping them with you—in which case, their containers become less coffins than vehicles for presentation. Clear resin or Lucite can offer both a final resting container and your display media: a scarab beetle or tarantula, for example, lightly coated in permanent plastic matter, makes a magnificent brooch or pendant; if you are lucky enough to have a pair of deceased pets, they lend themselves to use as striking shoe buckles or earrings, and will prove a real conversation point long after the mourning period is over.

Fig. 1. **Resin will preserve your pet "*au naturel*" for as long as you want to have them around.**

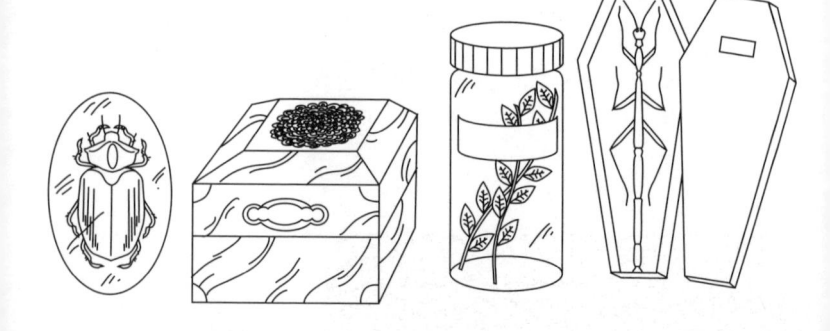

COFFINS FOR INSECTS

While beetles have a natural gleam and luster of their own, some other insect friends, once deceased, may benefit from a little borrowed finery. Bronzing or gilding will give them the presence they require to enhance an outfit, or simply to serve as an exquisite table center or dressing-table ornament. Companies that dip baby shoes will be happy to oblige: all you have to do is choose which metallic finish will best reflect the personality of your late pet, be it stick insect or hissing cockroach. It is an expensive alternative but your pet would not want you to be covered in guilt.

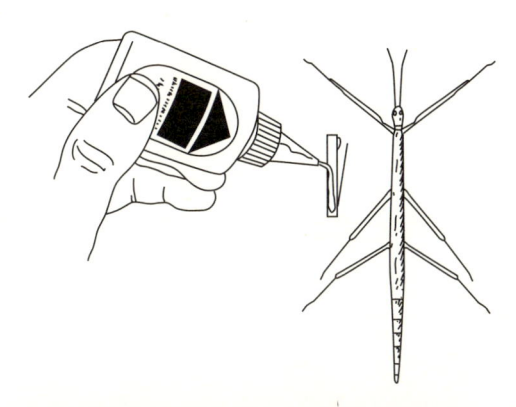

Fig. 2. Once gilded, your late friend can become a striking personal ornament. Just add a brooch fixing, pin it to your lapel, and you're set to go.

If you want to live and thrive,
Let the spider run alive.

Mid nineteenth-century proverb

COFFINS FOR REPTILES

The increasing popularity of snakes, lizards, and iguanas as pets will lead to a greater demand for custom-made services from pet funeral directors, who tend at present to focus on cats and dogs. However, though the professional undertaker currently falls short, it is perfectly possible for you to improvise a casket for your dead reptile from available materials.

Hatboxes will accommodate small, coiled snakes, and for particularly large specimens a pool cue case is ideal, enabling your pet to be displayed during the lying-in period. If the snake is too long to lie full-length in the case, simply fold the body back on itself as many times as is necessary. You will need to do this before rigor mortis sets in. For an interesting variation you could coil the body of the deceased around the length of the pool cue, thus lending a dynamic aspect to the lying-in period.

Snake- or crocodile-skin luggage is an obvious choice for reptiles, since it offers a dignified consistency of theme. It comes in a range of sizes, from a gentleman's

COFFINS FOR REPTILES

Fig. 1. The body of a snake should be arranged to match the length of the cue case.

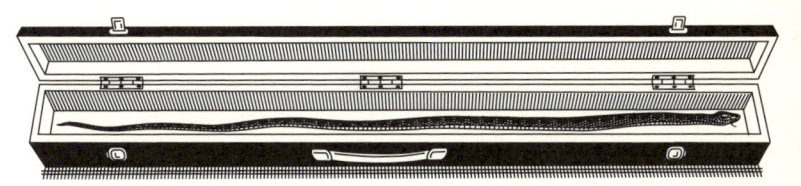

Fig. 2. The hinged lid means that it is a straightforward operation to display the deceased for visitors.

vanity case (suitable for a gecko or terrapin) to a valise (for a tortoise or iguana), or even a full-size suitcase (for exotica such as a sulcata tortoise or savannah monitor). Monogrammed in gold and lined with red or purple velvet, such an item offers a tasteful conveyance for your pet's last journey, with the added convenience of carrying handles, or even wheels. The ultimate in style...

CHOICE OF COFFIN

If your budget does not allow for snakeskin luggage, or if you would rather not bury your Louis Vuitton at the bottom of the garden, you can build a coffin from basic items. Choose a box appropriate to the size of the deceased and decorate it, matching the design to the departed creature. A terrapin or turtle would appreciate a casket with an aquatic theme, such as a simple box decorated with seashells or yellow flag iris, and lined with *Lagarosiphon major*. A taco box painted with skulls and filled with marigolds would be ideal for a green iguana, while a gecko would feel at home fixed to the underside of the coffin lid.

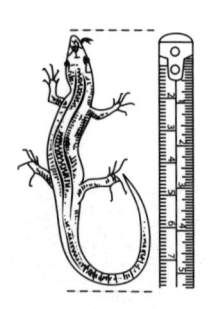

Fig. 1. You should take careful measurements of the deceased.

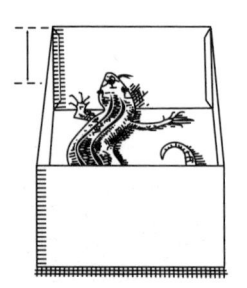

Fig. 2. The casket should be a neat fit without appearing cramped.

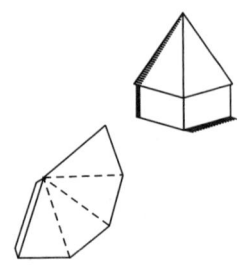

Fig. 3. You can create a variety of shapes using cardboard templates.

COFFINS FOR REPTILES

You could also construct a casket using cardboard folded to shape and glued, creating an interesting polyhedral structure that will have greater visual impact than a plain cuboid box. A pyramid or ziggurat shows even more imagination and is an appropriate final resting place for your exotic former companion. If you want to be eco-friendly and use natural materials rather than buy a textile lining, you could weave a litter from vine leaves or twigs; or carve a tomb from a piece of soft stone, such as pumice or soapstone, and lay out your reptile in his own private catacomb.

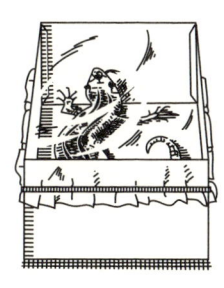

Fig. 4. **An acetate or clear plastic lid keeps the body from contamination while allowing the deceased to be viewed.**

*As if awakened,
she turns her face to yours;
and with shock,
you see yourself, tiny,
inside the golden amber
of her eyeballs
suspended, like a prehistoric fly.*

Rainer Maria Rilke, *"Black Cat"*

COFFINS FOR SMALL RODENTS

Mice, hamsters, and gerbils are the foot soldiers of the pet army. They are most popular as children's pets and have an average lifespan of between one and two years, so if you have children you can look forward to any number of poignant miniature ceremonies before the family is grown up. Look on every one of these little creatures as an opportunity to further perfect your expertise in throwing an elegant and moving pet funeral.

Just because the deceased was small, there's no need for a lack of imagination when it comes to his coffin. Many pass away naturally in a cutely curled position, and you can exploit and emphasize this in your choice of box or container. Consider a tennis-ball coffin (*as shown opposite*) or scour craft stores for small, round woven baskets that can be lined either with natural grass or hay or with shredded crêpe paper in pretty green or pale yellow shades. Depending on the time of year, you can sometimes find Easter favor baskets with lids, which can be sealed after the funeral and before the interment.

COFFINS FOR SMALL RODENTS

And if a basket also has a handle, the youngest family member can carry it solemnly to the graveside (although they should be warned that swinging the basket as they walk will not be appropriate on this occasion). Respect and reverence should be expected, if not demanded, even from younger mourners.

Fig. 1.

Fig. 2.

Fig. 3.

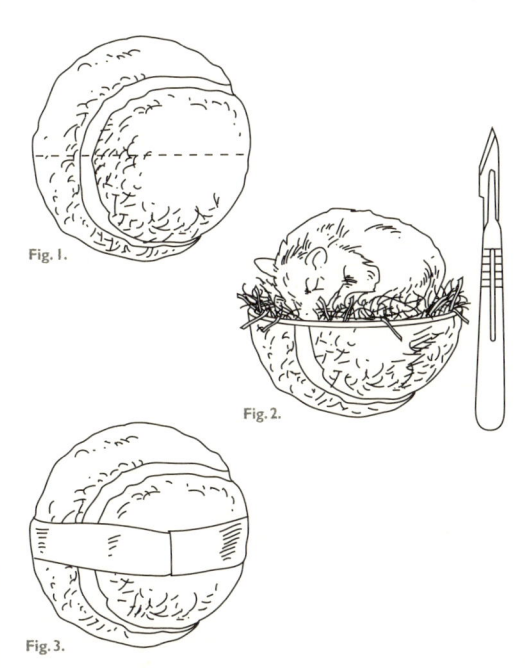

Fig. 1. Some wildlife organizations suggest using worn-out tennis balls as nesting sites for harvest mice. Instead, turn one into a site of perpetual rest for your mouse or hamster.

Fig. 2. Use a craft knife or very sharp scissors to cut a tennis ball neatly in half, then line one of the halves with wisps of hay. Arrange your late pet in a peaceful position on this rustic bed. A few wildflowers tucked around the edges give a charming effect.

Fig. 3. You can leave the ball-coffin open for a funeral viewing and close it afterward. When you wish to seal the coffin, simply tape it securely closed—duct tape will do a good, firm job.

CHOICE OF COFFIN

COFFINS FOR RABBITS AND LARGE RODENTS

When it comes to the passing of rabbits and larger rodents—chinchillas, guinea pigs, and rats—a shoebox, tastefully customized, is the classic container. Lined with hay or decorative grasses, and possibly with stenciled exterior decoration, even a plain box can make a fitting centerpiece for a moving little funeral. Pick your theme according to your taste: a spring-like motif is shown in the steps here, but you could equally choose a high-gloss black, varnished finish and add some brass handles (the type intended for a small chest of drawers will be about the right scale) for a stately effect. If you choose the latter option, a piece of gray or burgundy velvet would make an exquisite coffin lining.

Fig. 1. To turn an ordinary shoebox into a coffin worthy of your larger rodent, try a stenciled effect. Start by painting the exterior of both shoebox and lid white.

Fig. 2. A meadow scene is always fitting. Use a basic flower stencil to create a frieze of simple, yellow daisies. Add blades of green grass and leaves, and give each daisy a swaying stalk. You can buy or cut a stencil for these or paint them freehand.

Fig. 1.

Fig. 2.

COFFINS FOR RABBITS AND LARGE RODENTS

If you want an environmentally friendly coffin, you can make one with papier-mâché. The process is similar to that of making a piñata for a children's party. Tear up numerous sheets of newsprint and make a large bowl of paste from flour and water. Blow up a balloon to the right size for a coffin, and apply the paper and paste thickly in alternate layers. When the papier-mâché is about half an inch thick, leave the balloon on a flat surface to dry (this will give your coffin a flat base). It will be a day or two before it is ready to paint (your late friend may have to wait in the freezer for his custom-made coffin), but you can then cut it in half horizontally and paint it appropriately with poster paint.

Fig. 3.

Fig. 3. Stencil the flowers all around the edge of the box, about halfway up its sides. Add a daisy wreath on the box top. If you want a shiny coffin, you can use gloss varnish to give it a finishing touch.

COFFINS FOR FISH

Fish are perhaps the most problematic of all pets when it comes to dealing with the aftermath of death. To begin with, your relationship with a fish is complicated by the fact that you each pass your days in different media, with little opportunity for communion. You cannot hug your fish or stroke it, you cannot take it for walks or teach it to fetch sticks (though if you have the luxury of a pool, sharing a swim is entirely possible), and hand-feeding is similarly difficult. The expression "a cold fish" sums up the common perception of the emotional range of the piscine race, but it is nonetheless important not to deny your deep sense of loss at the death of your goldfish simply because others say that fish don't have any feelings. Allow others their opinions but do not be swayed by them. Your aquatic friend deserves as generous a send-off as any warm-blooded creature.

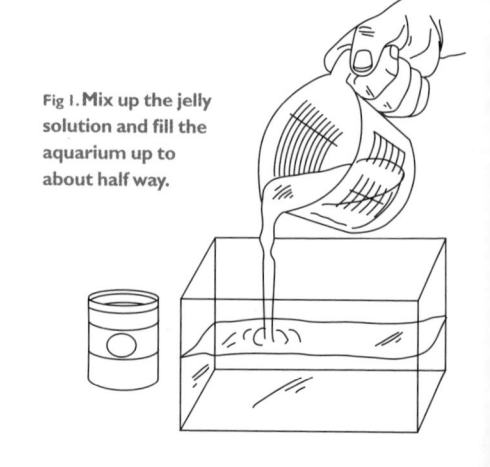

Fig 1. Mix up the jelly solution and fill the aquarium up to about half way.

COFFINS FOR FISH

This brings us to the second problem, namely that a dead fish represents something of a challenge to make presentable—in or out of water. The eyes stare blankly, the fins droop, and the scales quickly lose their luster. You need to work particularly fast with fish funeral arrangements. Keep the body wrapped in the fridge (carefully labeled) or in a cool place while you decide what preparations to make. One elegant solution is to display the deceased in a transparent tank suspended in agar jelly, a semisolid medium used to hold specimens in laboratory work. This material is nontoxic, easy to work with, and enables you to present your friend in a life-like "swimming" state for the period of lying-in and the funeral ceremony. Children will enjoy Sharky's suspended animation. After this, it is a simple task to remove the entire suspension for the interment.

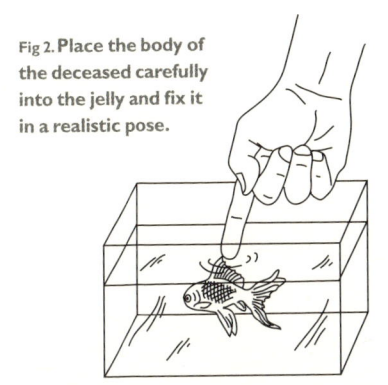

Fig 2. Place the body of the deceased carefully into the jelly and fix it in a realistic pose.

Fig 3. Fill the aquarium to the brim with the remainder of the jelly mixture to keep the deceased in position.

CHOICE OF COFFIN

If you dislike the idea of preserving your fish in aspic, or would prefer a more direct interaction with the deceased, it is advisable to take some care over laying out the body, so that your fish looks its best for the final ritual of its life. Keep in mind that you need to act quickly, because the ceremony will not be made any more bearable if the aroma of dead fish pervades the venue.

Spread out the fins, and glue small pieces of cheesecloth cut to shape to hold them open. To return the scales to their former shine, apply a light coat of metallic paint and let this dry before placing the deceased in the freezer until the funeral. Feel free to give Nature a hand and add extra glitter and tone. You should remove the body early enough to allow any ice crystals to melt. This is not cheating—it is simply lending dignity to your pet's leaving rites.

> *I think I could turn and live*
> *with animals, they are so placid*
> *and self-contained,*
> *I stand and look at them long and long.*
> Walt Whitman, *"Song of Myself"*

COFFINS FOR FISH

The casket should reflect the creature's natural environment. A toy wooden boat makes a good coffin for a large fish, while smaller and more colorful tropical varieties will be seen to good effect in an open clam shell. For a goldfish, a sardine tin lined with absorbent paper or fabric, and with the top partially rolled down, offers an ingenious resting place that enables mourners to view the deceased in appropriate surroundings. You could also use a layer of pond weed or a bed of shiny shells or small pebbles. You might even want to consider commissioning a portrait of your pet. Photographs remain the cheaper option, naturally.

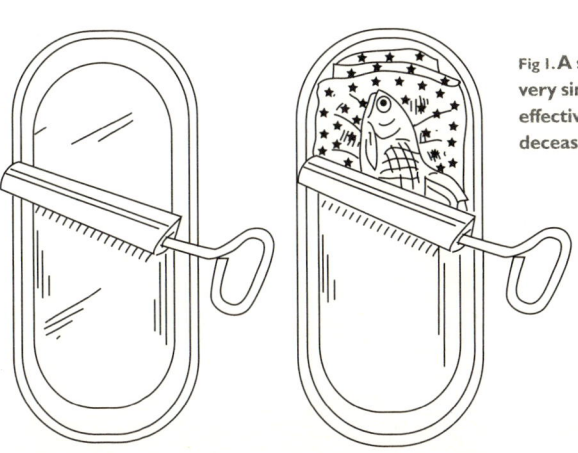

Fig 1. A sardine can is a very simple, witty, and effective casket for a deceased fish.

CHOICE OF COFFIN

COFFINS FOR CATS

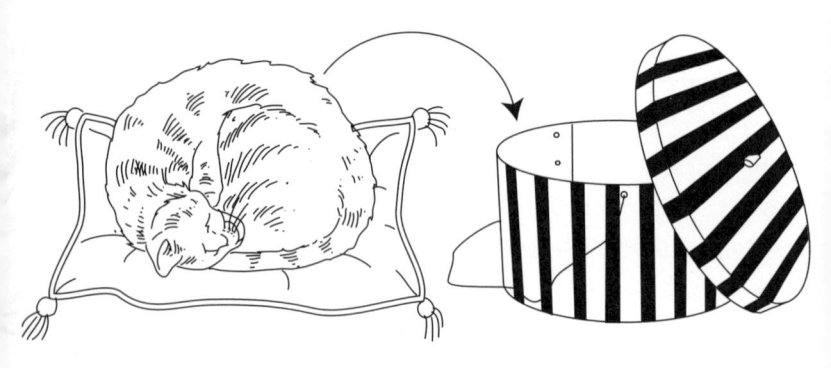

Fig. 1. **For the best effect, both pillow and cat should fit the hatbox as though it was made for them. Try posing your cat on the pillow before arranging both in the hatbox, to achieve the most comfortable and dignified effect.**

There are many ready-made boxes that may be appropriate for a deceased cat; as with larger reptiles, a hatbox will make a tasteful container in which to send your pet to natural-looking perpetual rest. Just make sure it is sturdy enough to take the weight, because hats are considerably lighter than cats. If your feline friend didn't pass away in a relaxed, curled position, make sure to pose him appropriately before rigor mortis sets in: blissfully rolled around with the tail neatly tucked under and apparently "asleep" on a downy pillow, a cat makes a lovely display in a large, shallow, circular box.

COFFINS FOR CATS

If you have artistic leanings, you could paint the exterior of the box with a suitable pattern, or cut out and adhere some images from a nature magazine. Running mice, prostrate birds, or creeping voles ready, perhaps, for consumption in the afterlife would all make appropriate decoration for the coffin of a famous hunter. Employing your creative skills might well help you with the grieving process.

If the hatbox proves too deep for an effective viewing, a false floor made from cardboard or balsa wood and raised on small blocks of wood will hold your pet at the appropriate level to allow the mourners to pay their last respects. A small circular cardboard frame with a picture of your cat in life might also be positioned centrally on the lid of the box, so that the image of the departed remains after the actual body is hidden from view.

I wonder what it is about a hat
That resembles so a lifeless cat?
Anonymous

CHOICE OF COFFIN

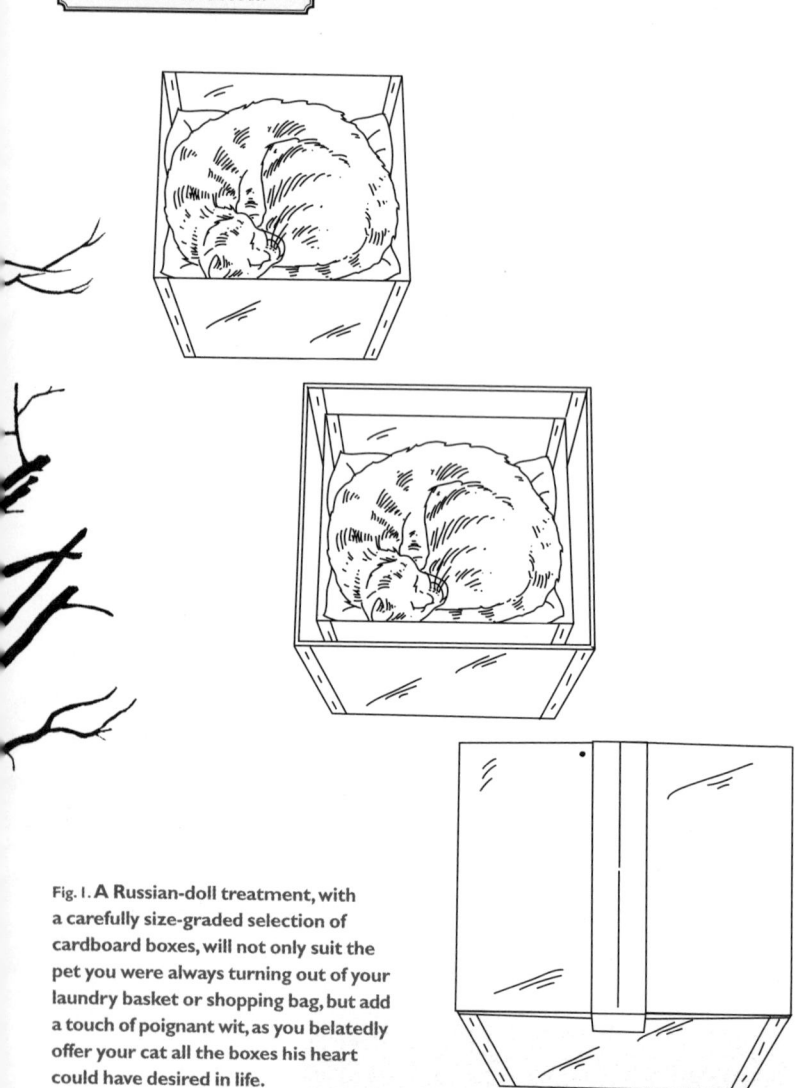

Fig. 1. A Russian-doll treatment, with a carefully size-graded selection of cardboard boxes, will not only suit the pet you were always turning out of your laundry basket or shopping bag, but add a touch of poignant wit, as you belatedly offer your cat all the boxes his heart could have desired in life.

COFFINS FOR CATS

In life, many cats love to hide or curl up for a nap in any large, empty cardboard box. You might decide that such a box could equally be a characteristic and suitable container for them in death. If, after some thought, you do choose to go down this simple route, a set of "nesting" boxes is easy to devise and will offer a more reverent and secure send-off than a single layer of cardboard.

First, find a square box that fits your cat snugly. Once your cat is inside, there should be little or no space around the body. Then find two or three boxes in which to fit the first container, sequentially, so that each box opens to reveal the one inside. Leave the top flaps of the boxes folded open for a viewing. Mourners will reap comfort from seeing the cat so comfortably contained.

There is no limit to the number of boxes you can use, but remember that a reverse "Pass the Parcel" effect after the funeral (since, in preparation for the interment, each of the boxes is taped up in turn) may spoil the solemn atmosphere that you've worked so hard to create.

A cardboard box makes a particularly suitable coffin for a feline friend that you believe to have had ecological leanings. If your pet was always lost in the contemplation of nature, or an incessant grass eater, you can comfort yourself with the thought that you've made the greenest of choices for his final resting place. For those whose concern for the environment matches that of the departed, the knowledge that you have done your bit for the threatened planet will bring extra solace.

No heaven will not ever Heaven be;
Unless my cats are there to welcome me.

Anonymous

CHOICE OF COFFIN

COFFINS FOR DOGS

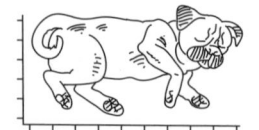

Fig. 1. Accurate measuring is essential before you order or start to construct a coffin.

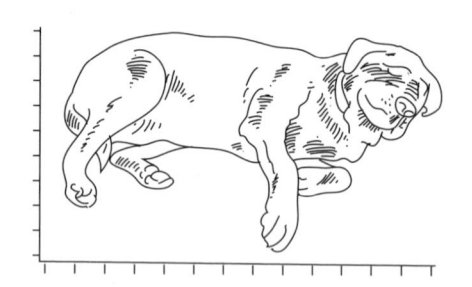

As the most popular type of pet, dogs are very well catered for by the professional pet funeral industry, with a range of caskets and urns available to convey their mortal remains into the afterlife. However, these containers are designed for the storage and conveyance of ashes after cremation (*see pages 100–101*). If you want your dog to pass over to the other side intact, then you are going to need something a bit larger. In this instance, size does indeed make a difference in a relationship, even though the latter has reached its physical conclusion.

First, measure your dog—an obvious thing to say, but unless you have the proper measurements, you will not know how large a coffin to order, or how

COFFINS FOR DOGS

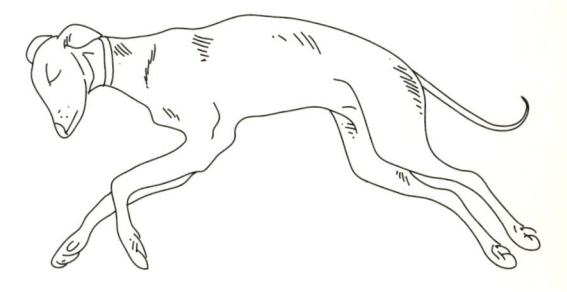

much material you will need if you are planning to make one yourself. If your late companion was a chihuahua, you are in luck, because a large shoebox makes a simple base for a coffin. On the other hand, if you were the owner of a mastiff or a Newfoundland, you have more of a problem and might well want to reconsider your decision against cremation.

Nonetheless, in all cases the principle is the same. It may help to lay the deceased on a large sheet of paper and draw roughly around the body, and then take measurements from that. If you are dealing with a large dog, be sure that the preservation of the body has been carried out thoroughly, because it will probably take you quite a while to complete the job in hand.

Fig. 2. **Lay out the body in a manner that reflects the characteristic pose of the animal in life.**

CHOICE OF COFFIN

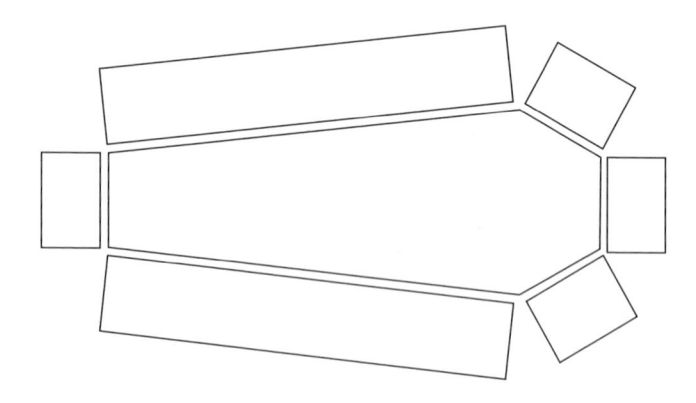

Fig. 1. Lay out all the necessary pieces for the coffin before you begin to fix them together so you can check for accuracy.

If you want a really good result, there is no alternative to hiring a professional cabinetmaker (unless you are a professional cabinetmaker). Simply supply the measurements and the check, and he will do the rest. However, if you value the personal touch over absolute squareness of corners and precision of joints—and assuming that you are not a complete bozo when it comes to power tools—do the job yourself.

Choose a timber that's easy to work with (so use pine over West African iroko), and cut the pieces as shown here to the relevant measurements. Remember to screw the sides to the edges of the base, rather than fixing the base to the lower edge of the sides, because

COFFINS FOR DOGS

then there will be less chance of the deceased falling through the bottom of the coffin when it's picked up (especially if he was on the large side). Line the casket (there is advice on this at the end of this chapter; *see pages 68–71*) and decorate the outside. You can paint the timber or cover it with bone-patterned wallpaper, or stencil your dog's name or stick blown-up photographs of the deceased onto it. Ask mourners to write a farewell message in crayon or chalk. Discourage graffiti. Fix brass handles to the casket or make geometric patterns by hammering round-headed nails into the sides.

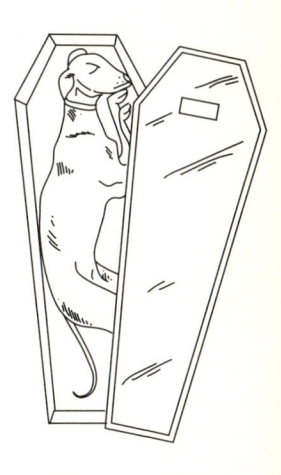

Fig. 2. You can attach a nameplate or a panel with a memorial inscription to the lid of the coffin before fixing it down.

Give free rein to your imagination and you will have a substantial tribute to your former companion, as well as gaining the confidence to deal with the garden gate yourself next time its hinges drop instead of paying good money to someone else.

> *He is your friend, your partner, your defender, your dog. You are his life, his love, his leader. He will be yours, faithful and true, to the last beat of his heart. You owe it to him to be worthy of such devotion.*
>
> Anonymous

CHOICE OF COFFIN

FINISHING AND LINING THE COFFIN

A well-finished coffin makes the most effective centerpiece for the funeral ceremony. Linings will naturally vary according to the pet—a pretty carpet of wheatgrass may suit a cat; a dog might be wrapped in his best blanket; a rabbit should be laid to rest on a comfortable bed of clean hay. Don't rule out plastic, which may be an ideal liner for an aquatic animal. The color against which your pet is placed is very much a matter of choice, too: an exquisite Persian cat's smoke-gray coat might look especially good against an extravagant lining of burgundy velvet, while a simpler lining of carefully arranged unbleached calico may be the best foil for the brilliant scales of a coral snake or the vivid plumage of a parakeet. This is an opportunity for you to make your own ultimate design statement.

> *A turkey carpet was his lawn,*
> *On which he loved to skip and bound,*
> *And leap and gambol like a fawn*
> *And swing his rump around.*
>
> William Cowper, *"Epitaph on a Hare"*

FINISHING AND LINING

Fig. 1. **Cotton, neatly draped, will look simple and natural.**

Fig. 2. **For a flamboyant finish, rich, deep-pile velvet makes a luxurious coffin lining.**

Fig. 3. **Artificial grass, in a brilliant, verdant green, is particularly suited to the smaller herbivorous pets.**

Fig. 4. **A high-gloss PVC can offer an effective backdrop for a natural water-dweller, such as a terrapin or newt.**

CHOICE OF COFFIN

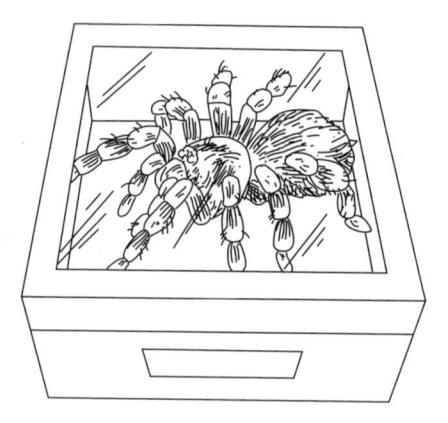

Fig. 1. An acetate lid is not only seemly and hygienic, but can also act as a potent symbol of the distance that now lies between you and your dead pet.

Broadly, the best rule of thumb to follow is: The more brilliant or lavish the coloring of the deceased, the more important it is to see them on a very neutral backdrop, which will set off their beauty more effectively. Less striking pets may need a little more help. One of the most beautiful coffin finishes we've ever seen was a case in which a small and homely hamster rested against a magnificent trim of saffron crêpe de chine.

> *Strength without Insolence,*
> *Courage without Ferocity,*
> *and all the virtues of Man without*
> *his Vices.*
>
> Lord Byron, *"Epitaph to a Dog"*

If you want to be able to view your companion, but prefer a hygienically closed coffin, a clear acetate top enables viewings while acting as a seal on the box. Presenting your late loved one in a closed container also offers the opportunity for a plaque on the coffin lid. This type of exterior coffin ornament depends entirely on your taste and artistic ability.

A small label with the deceased's name and dates is a nice touch, and can be made from cardboard or wood, depending on your choice of medium for the coffin. If you want to impress your friends and increase the gravitas of this last meeting with your pet, a Latin tag or motto might also be suitable. Choose carefully. *Amor vincit omnia* ("Love conquers all") may seem simply untrue in the face of death, but *Peritus sed non oblitus* ("Gone, but not forgotten") would be appropriate for any pet of any species. Cut the plaque to a simple shape, and practice your calligraphy on a piece of paper cut to the same size, before writing on the real thing. It would be easy, upsetting, and potentially costly, to make a mistake on the final plaque, so take your time to get it just right. There is no rush.

Fig. 2. This isn't the place for a full-length epitaph. Save your more long-winded thoughts for the speeches, and aim for a pithy economy of sentiment when it comes to the coffin top.

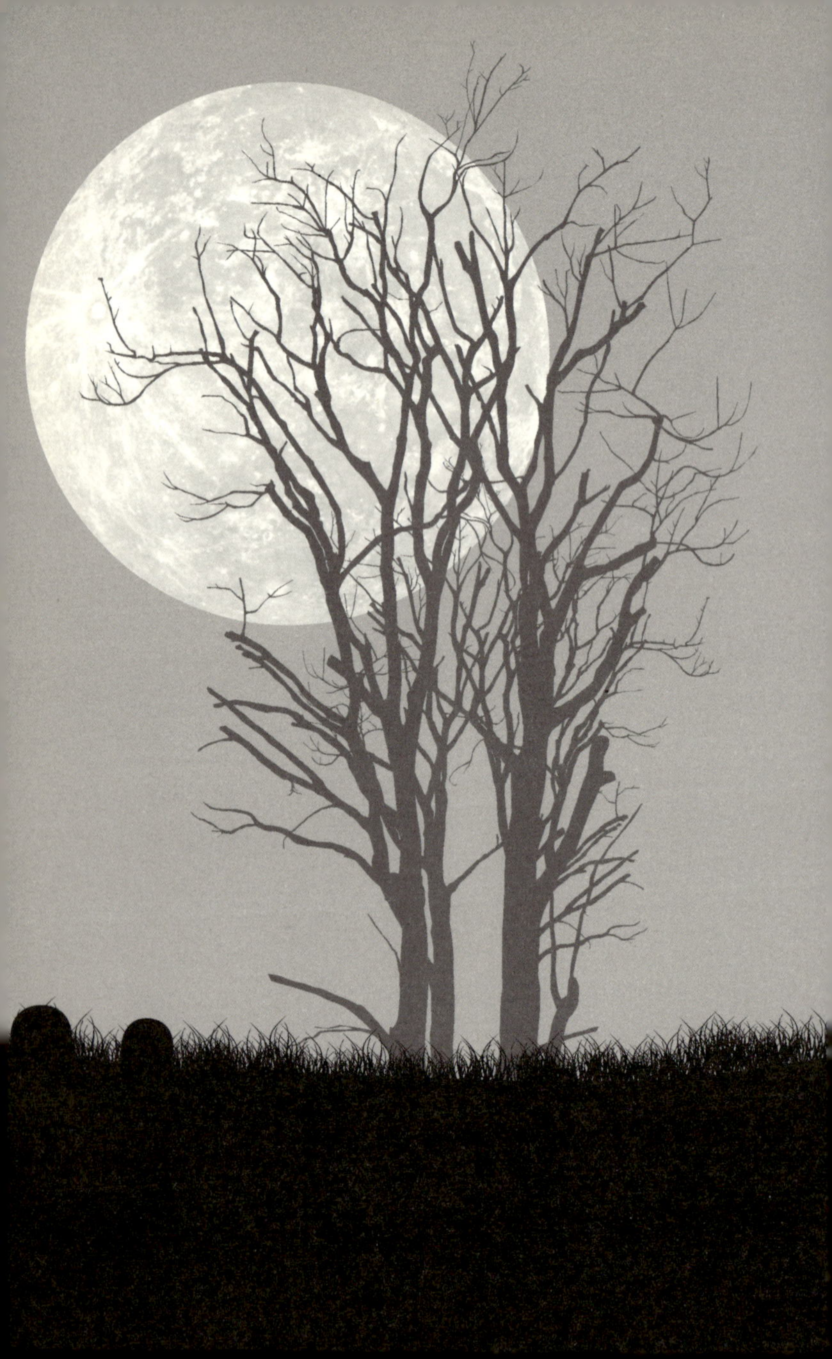

THE FUNERAL

VIGILS AND WAKES

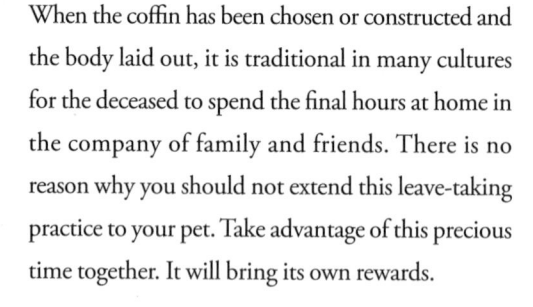

When the coffin has been chosen or constructed and the body laid out, it is traditional in many cultures for the deceased to spend the final hours at home in the company of family and friends. There is no reason why you should not extend this leave-taking practice to your pet. Take advantage of this precious time together. It will bring its own rewards.

Set the coffin on a low table in your best reception room, and place candles at the head and foot of the bier. Arrange some flowers in a vase behind the coffin. You might want to have some appropriate music playing in the background, perhaps something the deceased was particularly fond of. If your pet had a large number of friends and relatives, you may want to consider an extended lying-in period so that everyone has a chance to pay their respects (although this does assume a degree of confidence in your embalming skills). If your pet was a party animal, you might even decide to follow the Jamaican nine-nights tradition with singing and dancing and quantities of rum.

However, it is perfectly acceptable to have a small family affair with simple refreshments, and to spend these last hours together sharing informal reminiscences about your late pet. If you are attending the vigil on your own, it is a good idea to have a book of poetry or some other contemplative reading on hand. With the funeral arrangements now in place, this is a time for quiet reflection on the joyful times that you shared and the happiness you gave each other. This is one of life's most intense and intimate moments.

Fig. I. **No pet is so small as to be unworthy of a tasteful presentation during his final hours in your household.**

FLORAL TRIBUTES

Fig. 1. **Did you love your pet or did you not? Say it with daisies.**

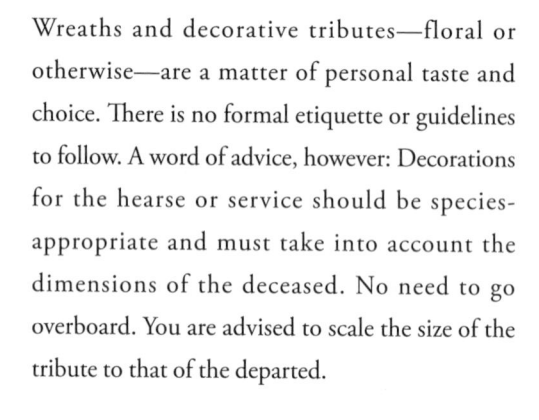

Fig. 2. **Don't limit yourself to floral tributes. Other natural ingredients could be more appropriate, such as seaweed, straw, or salad leaves, used as fresh as possible.**

Wreaths and decorative tributes—floral or otherwise—are a matter of personal taste and choice. There is no formal etiquette or guidelines to follow. A word of advice, however: Decorations for the hearse or service should be species-appropriate and must take into account the dimensions of the deceased. No need to go overboard. You are advised to scale the size of the tribute to that of the departed.

In the animal kingdom, as in the larger natural world, simple designs often have the greatest visual impact. A daisy wreath for a guinea pig, or a lettuce garland for a tortoise—both suggestions combine simplicity, poignancy, and subtlety to perfect effect. A bunch of large white lilies perched precariously upon a hearse for a mouse could easily diminish the true sentiment of the event. You might think of using a single *Strelitzia* (bird-of-paradise flower) to mirror a deceased parrot in color, size, and indeed possibly origin. A seaweed wreath would make a fitting farewell for a fish or terrapin.

FLORAL TRIBUTES

To convey the personality of the deceased, you may wish to go down a more symbolic route. If your dog had a healthy appetite and a sense of humor, why not assemble a bone-shaped wreath made of his favorite dog biscuits? Wit and imagination can both play a role in decorative tributes. Donations to a local rescue center or appropriate charities can replace floral tributes for those who decide against them.

Fig. 3. **Be inventive with your wreath. Shape up to the occasion.**

Fig. 4. **For those averse to flowers, a charity collection box is a good alternative. Use your children's piggy bank in extremis.**

THE FUNERAL

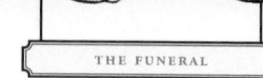

HEARSES

Fig. 1. Arranging to have the hearse drawn by close companions of the deceased is a charming way for the final journey to take place.

At its simplest, a hearse is a means of getting the coffin from the deceased's home to the funeral and the place of interment. In many cases you could perfectly well carry the coffin, but a wheeled vehicle lends a degree of gravitas to the final journey.

If your pet is remaining in the bosom of your family at the end of the backyard or garden, consider adapting a child's wagon with black crepe and plumes, to convey the coffin to the funeral ceremony and then to the final resting place. If the journey is further afield, you could use the family automobile (assuming that you are not sending off a favorite horse), though you should dignify the vehicle with black ribbons. However, if this strikes you as rather prosaic, arrange to borrow a flatbed cart, such as those used for moving luggage at airports.

Better still, and assuming that the deceased is sufficiently small, arrange for the hearse to be drawn by other animals, preferably friends of the late pet. The terriers that used to cavort with your well-loved cat may be pleased to have a final opportunity to enjoy his company. Harnesses can be made from upholstery tape, while ostrich-feather headdresses will lend an air of grandeur to the proceedings.

> *Thou who passest on the path, if happily
> thou dost mark this monument,
> Laugh not, I pray thee,
> Though it is a dog's grave,
> tears fell for me, and the dust was heaped
> above me by a master's hand,
> who likewise engraved these
> words upon my tomb.*
>
> J.W. Mackail, "*Epigrams from the Greek Anthology*"

THE FUNERAL PROCESSION

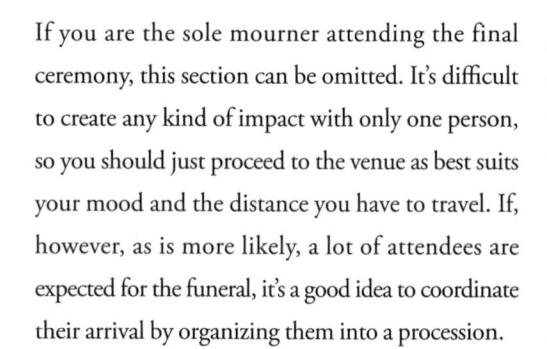

If you are the sole mourner attending the final ceremony, this section can be omitted. It's difficult to create any kind of impact with only one person, so you should just proceed to the venue as best suits your mood and the distance you have to travel. If, however, as is more likely, a lot of attendees are expected for the funeral, it's a good idea to coordinate their arrival by organizing them into a procession.

You should ask the mourners to gather early at the departure point, and give some thought in advance to the best processional order. Assuming that the venue is within walking distance, ask one person to act as the advance guard, walking in front of the hearse with a bell to attract the attention of bystanders. You should follow as chief mourner, with close family and then friends following on. If other pets are in attendance, you will want to ensure that natural predators (or pets that have a history of indisposition toward each other) are kept apart, so as to avoid any danger of the solemnities degenerating into an unseemly fracas.

THE FUNERAL PROCESSION

Alternatively, if you want the proceedings to be more light-hearted or celebratory, you could follow the New Orleans custom of jazz funerals. If you don't have the services of a jazz band, ask mourners, particularly children, to bring along musical instruments and play the deceased out in style. Those who can't play can clap along.

Fig. 1. The mourners in the funeral procession should be ranked according to their intimacy with the deceased and size relative to each other.

> *Love the animals:*
> *God has given them the rudiments*
> *of thought and joy untroubled.*
> Fyodor Dostoyevsky

THE FUNERAL

ORDER OF SERVICE

It is important to decide well in advance on the content and order of the service to be held for your departed companion. Discuss with family and friends who should speak when and, importantly, for how long. Those closest to the deceased and those who feel the loss most intensely should take priority.

Choose between a brief yet moving service, itself perhaps a reflection of the life of the deceased, and a lengthier, more involved service with several participants and rather more fulsome speeches. A printed order of service is a nice touch and avoids distressing confusion during a time of still rather raw grief. If—by misfortune or sad coincidence—you lose two members of your animal household at the same time, a joint service is a convenient option and can be a memorable, cathartic experience that kills two birds with one stone.

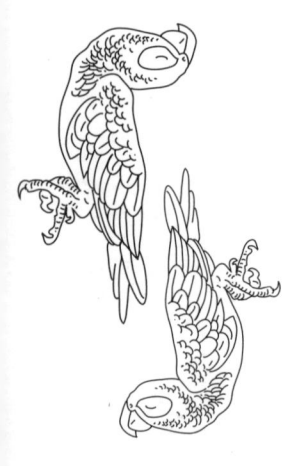

Fig. 1. **Every cloud has a silver lining. You can kill two birds with one stone and turn the misfortune of losing two pets into an advantage, by holding a joint funeral.**

> *Heaven goes by favor; if it went by merit, you would stay out and your dog would go in.*
>
> Mark Twain

ORDER OF SERVICE

Music is a good idea for the beginning of the service when people are wondering where to sit, and also at the end while the coffin is being borne from the ceremony. The wealthy and well connected may find solace in commissioning a special piece of music for the event and invite a professional to sing a customized aria. Alternatively, arrange for your children to practice, perfect, and perform a favorite hymn or song. If your dog was given to tuneless howling at classical music, ask members of the local school orchestra to deliver a rendition of Schubert's "Trout Quintet." In the absence of large funds, great influence, or small children, play a CD of music that was enjoyed with the deceased on long car rides.

Fig. 2. Get your children to pay a musical tribute to the departed. "All things bright and beautiful, All creatures great and small" would be suitable, whereas "How much is that doggy in the window?" is more fitting for farewells featuring younger family members.

EULOGIES AND READINGS

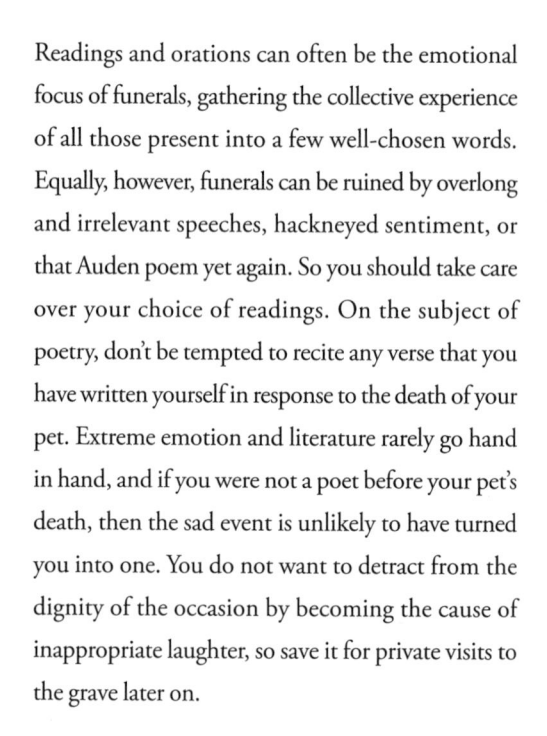

Readings and orations can often be the emotional focus of funerals, gathering the collective experience of all those present into a few well-chosen words. Equally, however, funerals can be ruined by overlong and irrelevant speeches, hackneyed sentiment, or that Auden poem yet again. So you should take care over your choice of readings. On the subject of poetry, don't be tempted to recite any verse that you have written yourself in response to the death of your pet. Extreme emotion and literature rarely go hand in hand, and if you were not a poet before your pet's death, then the sad event is unlikely to have turned you into one. You do not want to detract from the dignity of the occasion by becoming the cause of inappropriate laughter, so save it for private visits to the grave later on.

It's best if those chosen to read are accustomed to speaking in public, and they should of course have rehearsed the reading in advance. We have made some suggestions for appropriate poetry or prose extracts to lend gravitas to the ceremony.

EULOGIES AND READINGS

Gerard Manley Hopkins' "Pied Beauty" makes a splendid funeral piece for a calico cat.

William Blake's "The Tyger" would suit a tabby that liked hunting.

Rudyard Kipling's "The Power of the Dog" distills the very essence of the bond between human and canine.

Robert Burns' "To a Mouse" serves admirably for any kind of rodent, though you may wish to supply an English translation

Marianne Moore's "The Pangolin" is probably not much in demand, but it's useful to know it is there, should you need it.

THE FUNERAL

PAGAN RITES

If neither you nor your ex-pet subscribes to Western religious ideas about death and the afterlife, but you nonetheless view the deceased as more than simply a piece of meat, a ritual that marks the natural cycle of birth and death might be comforting.

Fig. 1. **Choose an appropriate outdoor setting for a pagan funeral to encourage a sense of return to nature.**

Pagan services are best suited to the outdoors, and to woodland sites in particular, where the spirit of the Earth Goddess can be most strongly felt. Mark out the ceremonial space with candles or lanterns, and decorate the area with flowers. Light some incense sticks and place the deceased at the center of the space. Attendees at pagan funerals traditionally wear white to symbolize joy at the return of the deceased to the natural element. You should bring a large bowl of clean water so that celebrants can purify their hands as they arrive, and some sprigs of rosemary for

Hoof and Horn, Hoof and Horn,
All That Dies Shall Be Reborn.
Corn and Grain, Corn and Grain,
All That Falls Shall Rise Again.

Ian Corrigan

PAGAN RITES

each person to hold. It is a good idea to ask mourners to play drums or sing, to create a mellow atmosphere before the ritual begins. When everyone has arrived, they should all join hands to form a circle around the deceased. The circle should remain unbroken until the ceremony is complete. What is then said depends on your own inclinations. You may wish to invoke the spirit of the Earth to take the deceased back to her, you may want to share some memories of the deceased, or you may simply wish to stand in silent communion with the natural world. It is a good idea to close the ceremony with a traditional pagan chant, such as the one opposite. Then the circle can be parted and the cremation or burial can take place.

Fig. 2. White magic can be a powerful comforting force at a time of bereavement.

HUMANIST FUNERALS

For the recently bereaved who decide against a religious service, a humanist funeral provides a suitably secular send-off for pets that have shuffled off this mortal coil. For atheists, agnostics, and those more resolute in their desire for a nonreligious service than one in any faith, a humanist service is a celebration of a life in retrospect. Its primary goal is to capture the essence of the deceased's personality rather than offering any misguided hope of reunion in the hereafter.

Take advantage of the perfect opportunity to highlight the greatest achievements and virtues of the departed, along with his contribution to the family, or indeed wider society. Focus on the joy, comfort, assistance, and laughter your ex-pet brought you and those sharing in the celebration. There should be nothing to offend those less comfortable with nonreligious funerals; indeed, they should enjoy listening to (preferably) short anecdotes, prepared and written in advance for smooth delivery on the day, about prizes won (at village, national, or international level), rewarding friendships forged with household members—two- or four-legged—or lives assisted, saved, and enriched in a number of ways.

You might choose to invite a humanist celebrant to preside over affairs, but ensure that you inform them of the key character traits and memorable events that marked the life you are there to celebrate. Finish with a moment's silence, during which each of those present fixes in his or her mind for eternity the personality of the dead pet.

HUMANIST FUNERALS

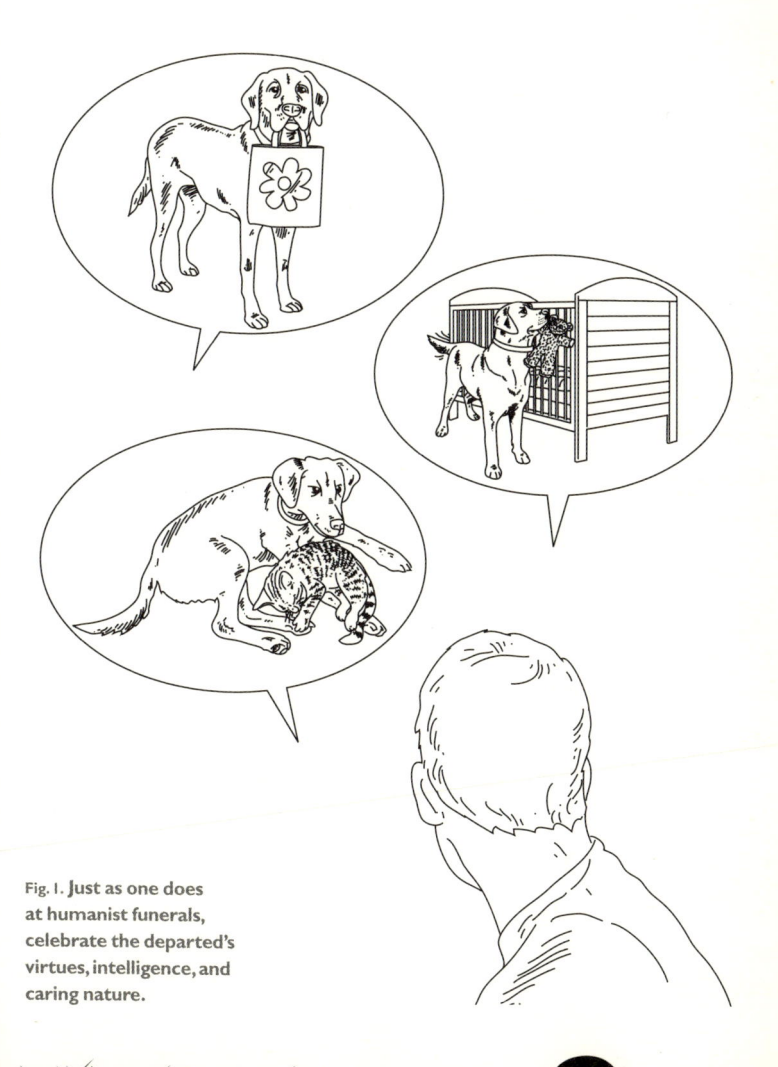

Fig. 1. **Just as one does at humanist funerals, celebrate the departed's virtues, intelligence, and caring nature.**

THE FUNERAL

PERSONALIZING THE RITES

Fig. 1. **Play a piece dedicated to your pet's own unique vocal skills.**

As a recently bereaved owner, you will be only too keenly aware of the singularity of your former companion. No two pets, like no two humans, are identical. This applies to the service to commemorate them, as indeed it does to the grieving process itself (*see page 114*). There is no shame in celebrating the individuality of your pet with a service specifically tailored to reflect it, highlighting his attributes and idiosyncrasies. It is not a "one size fits all" occasion.

Take time to decide upon ways to make the event peculiar to the deceased. If your canary liked cooing, karaoke-style, to particular songs, engage a group of singers, or an aspiring pop diva within the extended family, to pay appropriate tribute to his vocal skills. Play a pre-recording of a passed-on parrot to introduce the hymns or say a few words to those gathered to say goodbye.

PERSONALIZING THE RITES

Fig. 2. Dogs hear sounds we find inaudible. Although this does not work in reverse, invite your pet's canine companions to join in a song to commemorate the departed.

Commemorate a hamster that enjoyed going full circle in his cage by commissioning an acrobatic display by younger mourners (the fitter owner could perform this personally in the absence of same). A local circus troupe could be engaged if you felt your pet was particularly adept at tricks and turns. If Rex was inclined to less than fine whining to Elvis, ask an aspiring musician within the family to play "You Ain't Nothing but a Hound Dog" while other dogs howl along in similarly unrhythmic fashion. Professional or amateur canine choirs are an option for those with the necessary time and training.

Until one has loved an animal,
a part of one's soul remains unawakened.
Anatole France

THE FUNERAL

Apply creativity not only to the content of the service, but also to its actual venue, in order to personalize the event. Try to think outside the box. For those who have lost a fish—whether a simple, yet much-loved goldfish or a more exotic type such as the *Betta splendens* or Siamese fighting fish, or even a larger, more impressive carp—an open-air ceremony, with suitable waterproof and weather-proof attire provided for those attending, could be held around a pond, public or private, or indeed a swimming pool (with the necessary permissions in place). In this way those present can appreciate more fully the life lived and now lost.

Hilltop services for a dog that enjoyed long uphill hikes at your side are also an option, depending upon the fitness of the guests and the amount of equipment required. A less strenuous service for a feline companion could be held in a circle in the warmth and comfort of your living room, with the guests relaxing on cushions. Holding the ceremony in a place with symbolic or actual significance for the deceased will add meaning and sentiment to the occasion and will ensure it is long remembered.

PERSONALIZING THE RITES

Additional sentimental and visual impact can be injected by including a photograph of the deceased on the order of service, and posters displayed tastefully around the walls or at the entrance. Ask those attending to sign a remembrance book and to add a comment about their particular memory of your late companion. Younger members might like to sport clothing—a T-shirt perhaps—featuring a likeness of the pet. The possibilities presented for personalizing the event are, unlike the lifespan of the pet in question, endless.

Fig. 1. **What better way to pay respect to your recently departed pet than with a tasteful T-shirt, which can then be worn at later memorials?**

THE FUNERAL

HOLDING A RECEPTION

No matter how awful you are feeling, it's important to offer mourners some hospitality and refreshments after the ceremony. You might even find that you enjoy the event, as a celebration of the life that has passed, particularly if you did not hold a wake beforehand. Emotional experiences are physically and mentally draining, and it may well be that your guests have traveled some distance to attend, so you should provide a good spread. As everyone relaxes and unwinds, you may be offered some valuable and comforting insights into the influence that your former companion had on the lives of your friends.

Tailor the food to the guests and the event. Canapés and sandwiches are fine for the humans, and you could make some pet-shaped cookies or a decorated cake as a charming reminder of the deceased. (Be careful not to take this too far, however; Peeps might cause unnecessary upset to a young person who has lost a bunny, while serving hot dogs at the reception for a dachshund might seem like a good idea at the time, but would be in very poor taste.)

HOLDING A RECEPTION

Don't forget the animal mourners: Crudités for the herbivores, meaty chews and biscuits for the dogs, catnip bites and dried fish for the felines, mixed nuts and maize for the rodents. They should have easy access to the outdoors. Alcohol is best served to human mourners only.

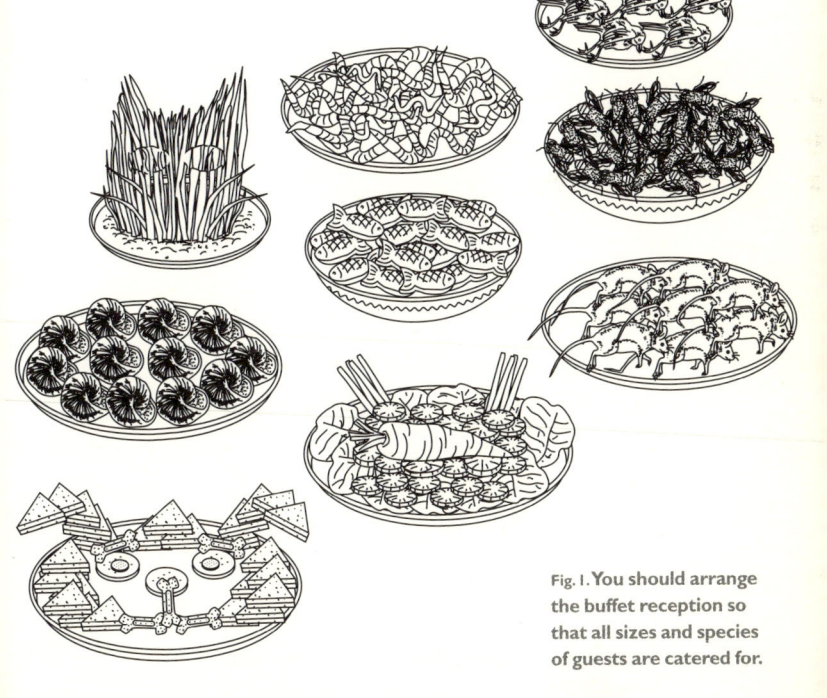

Fig. 1. You should arrange the buffet reception so that all sizes and species of guests are catered for.

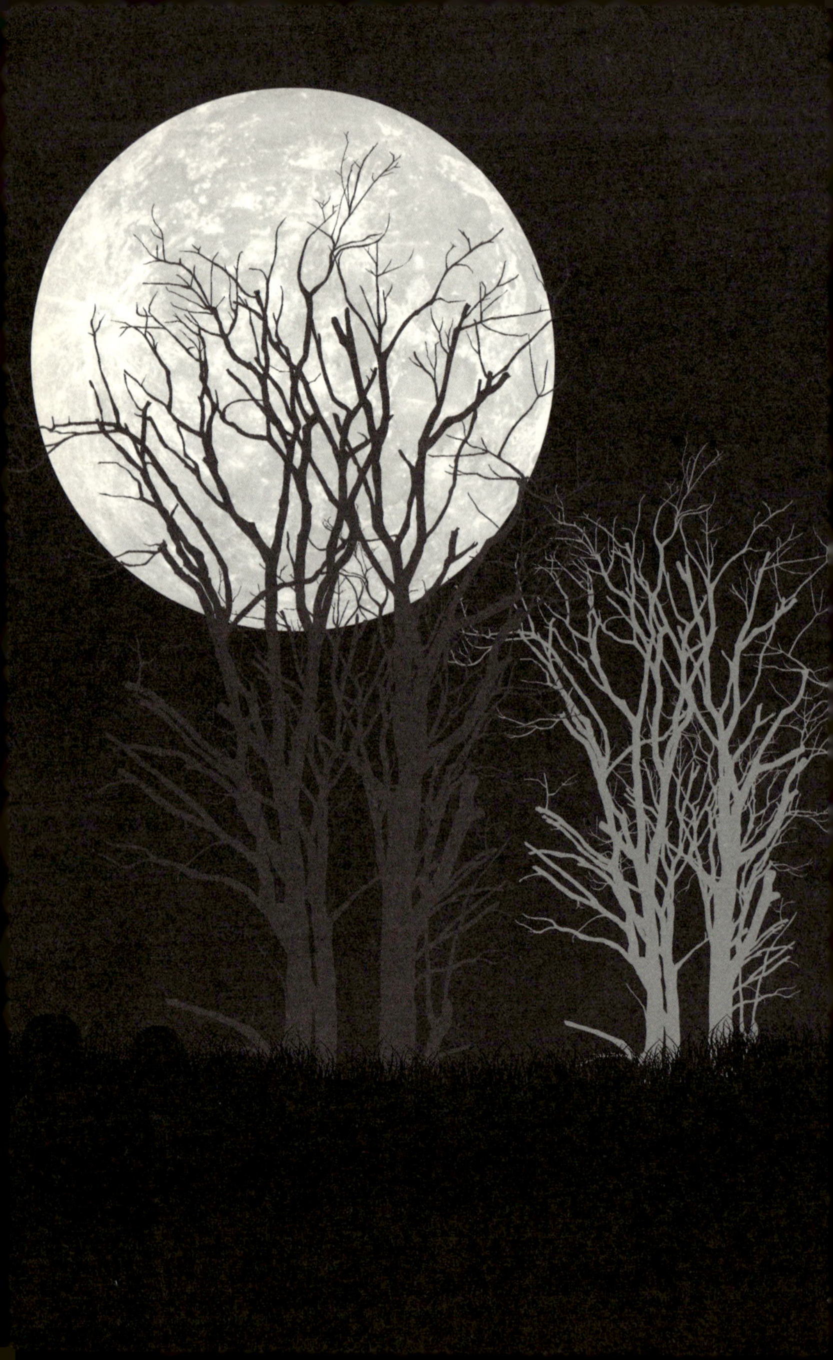

THE INTERMENT

THE INTERMENT

FAMILY GRAVES

For those whose yard and whose plans for its long- or medium-term ownership allow, a personal pet paradise offers an excellent solution to the grave issue. There's no place like home, even for the deceased.

In order to accommodate your late pet in perpetuity in your own backyard, first select a peaceful corner—with care. Make its position and perimeter clear, to avoid unwitting or thoughtless reuse by others as a composting or play area. Mark out your territory, perhaps using a white picket fence with a small gate to ensure both privacy and protection. Plant it with bushes and flowers. You might choose a rose with a meaningful name (Don Juan for a rabbit, for example, or Sexy Rexy for a dog with many descendants), or use a hole much favored by your pet in which to plant it.

Naturally, the size of the graveyard will depend upon the number of pet remains that have passed through your hands (and your plans for more), but as your companions fall off their mortal perch, they can

FAMILY GRAVES

follow each other into familiar ground. The goal is to create a sanctuary, a tranquil spot for remembrance and reflection, for you and future generations of your human (and animal) family. You may want to name it. You could also build or commission a bench bearing the names and dates of the various pets. Incorporate statues or sculptures as concrete reminders of, and tributes to, your pets. This is a place to sit and stare, contemplate, and commemorate and to reflect on the unceasing cycle of birth and death.

Fig. 1. **A well-tended memorial garden is a thing of beauty and a joy forever.**

THE INTERMENT

CREMATION

Cremation is perhaps the most hassle-free method of dealing with the mortal remains of your pet, and is ideal for busy people who may not have the leisure time to make coffins from old hatboxes or design complicated floral arrangements. Many veterinarians offer a collection service and will take away the body of the deceased and return you a neat package that you can dispose of as you wish. You should get written confirmation in advance that your pet is the only one you will get back, since mass cremation is not uncommon and one lot of ash looks much like another. You will want to avoid expending a great

Fig. 1. **After cremation the ashes of your former companion can be scattered wherever you feel to be most appropriate.**

CREMATION

deal of emotional energy over the remains of a random assortment of other people's hamsters, cats, and parrots.

Having your pet's remains cremated offers a number of advantages. It enables you to preserve the deceased in a handy pouch and take him with you wherever you go, should you so wish, thus retaining the companionship that meant so much to you before. Or you can deposit the ashes in a distinctive urn or other vessel that would make a striking centerpiece for dinner parties. Cremation also means that you can lay your pet to rest discreetly in a place that might otherwise be inaccessible or inadvisable. Perhaps your cat particularly enjoyed hunting in your neighbors' garden, for instance, and scattering the ashes there means that he can spend eternity in his favorite place. If you wait until your neighbors are out it can be a final shared secret between you and your pet. Be careful to scatter them widely, however, because if you drop half a pound of calcium phosphate directly onto your neighbor's azaleas, you will not be popular.

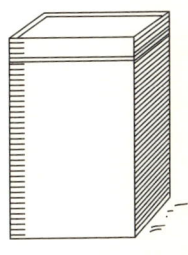

Fig. 2. The ashes will be returned by the vet in a simple box, but you can then place them in any container you like.

THE INTERMENT

SEA BURIAL

Fig. 1. Weight the coffin, and ensure it is tightly closed before placing it carefully into the boat.

Fig. 2. Lower the coffin slowly over the side using tapes wrapped around each end.

Fig. 3. When the coffin reaches the water, release the tapes.

This is a dignified way to say goodbye to an aquatic pet (or even a land-based pet that was especially fond of water). If the deceased was cremated, you can scatter the ashes into a favorite river or lake, either from the bank or from a boat. Read some suitable words—a Bible passage perhaps or some poetry—and strew some flower petals out onto the surface of the water. It goes without saying that you should always check which way the wind is blowing before scattering the ashes, because the moment (and whatever outfit you are wearing) will be ruined if the deceased is simply blown back at you. There is also the danger of inadvertent inhalation, which should be avoided at all costs.

If you want to bury a coffin in water, you will need to weight it first—there is nothing more disheartening than having to pursue a coffin that you were attempting to consign to the deep, while it bobs merrily on the waves or gets caught up with fishing lines and overhanging branches. Place some stones or a brick inside the coffin, close it securely,

SEA BURIAL

Fig. 4. **A fiery vessel offers a dramatic finale for an adventurous pet.**

and then lower the burden into the water by means of bands. When the coffin reaches the water, you can release the bands at each end and let it slide quietly beneath the waves.

For a grander exit, assuming that you have access to a large expanse of open water, adopt the Viking method and dispatch your companion to Valhalla in a blazing vessel. Use a wooden boat and soak it well with some inflammable fuel such as paraffin. Push it away from the bank before igniting it; again take care to check the wind direction, or alternatively invite a sympathetic firefighter to the ceremony.

THE INTERMENT

SKY BURIAL

In Native American and Tibetan culture, a sky burial is one in which the body is left out in the open for predators to dispose of naturally. We described it under the less romantic title of excarnation earlier in this book (*see pages 36–37*). Unless you have a large and barren desert on your doorstep, this will not be practical for most domestic disposals, and you may anyway have decided that this ritual is a bit too natural for your taste. You can, however, make a cultural nod to the idea

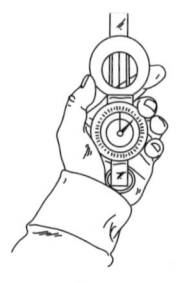

Fig. 1. **Always check the wind direction before lighting an open fire.**

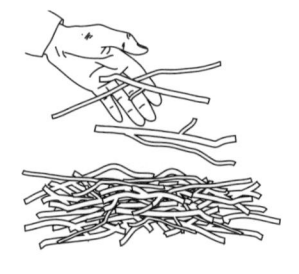

Fig. 2. **Make a pile of combustible material big enough for the deceased.**

Fig. 3. **Lie the body carefully on top of the pyre.**

Fig. 4. **When the blaze is complete the ashes can be retrieved.**

by cremating your pet yourself, in the open, and letting his mortal remains dissipate into the ether.

If you have ever built a bonfire, the same principles apply. You will need enough dry timber to produce a good blaze—take into account the size of the deceased when gathering combustible material. First, set the coffin on a wooden bench or table and stack the timber around it. As before (*see page 102*), check the wind direction before ignition and make sure that the mourners are all upwind of the funeral pyre.

If you are extremely wealthy it is possible to arrange to have your pet's remains put into orbit around the Earth, so that they can shine down on you from the starry firmament.

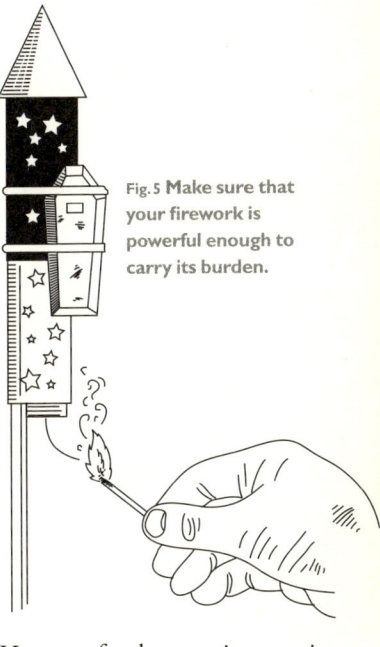

Fig. 5 **Make sure that your firework is powerful enough to carry its burden.**

However, for the more impecunious, fireworks offer much the same result. The ashes of small pets, such as mice or goldfish, can be readily attached to skyrockets and launched into the happy hunting grounds—an exciting and visually dramatic way to bow out.

GRAVE GOODS

In China there is a tradition of making cardboard and paper facsimiles of money, clothing, possessions, cars, and, indeed, houses to provide comfort and assistance to the deceased in the afterlife. A ritual burning of such objects subsequently takes place, in order for such goods to head with the dead to the hereafter. It is a fascinating and often spectacular ceremony, and you might want to consider including it in the farewell for a furry friend.

Follow the clear instructions shown opposite to design, cut out, and assemble a simple dog house for your canine companion, using plain paper or cardboard. You can adapt the size and shape to mirror more sophisticated lodgings, or indeed to design homes for other species; constructing a cage, aquarium, or basket should not present too great a challenge. Paint and accessorize the final construction accordingly if time, inspiration, and artistic skill allow. You might even find solace in the inclusion of paper replicas of such extras as toys and perhaps a favored pillow or cushion, to make the afterlife as comfortable as possible, bearing in mind that all your efforts are destined to go up in flames. Set fire to the facsimile home with great care and solemnity, ensuring that all mourners, especially those of a tender age, are at a suitably safe distance. The ceremony should be comforting and cathartic. Take a photograph for posterity—you might like to include it in a journal (*see page 115*) or memory book, or show it to fellow pet-owning friends who might be unfortunate enough to lose companions in the future. Do not share your new knowledge with anyone showing the slightest hint of pyromania.

GRAVE GOODS

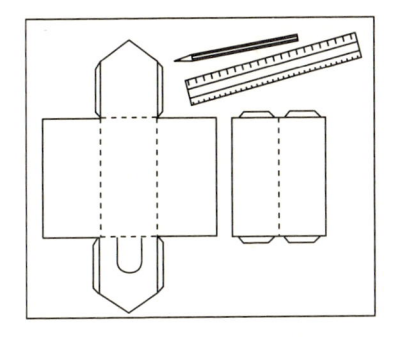

Fig. 1. **Use paper or cardboard to make the dog house, adapting its dimensions according to the size of your pet.**

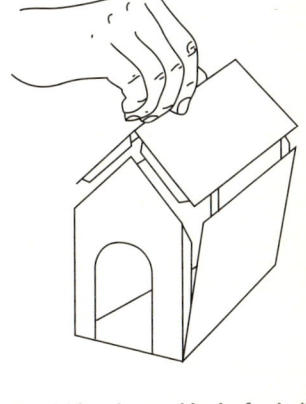

Fig. 2. **Cut, fold, and assemble the facsimile with care and precision. Accessorize if time, skill, or temperament allow.**

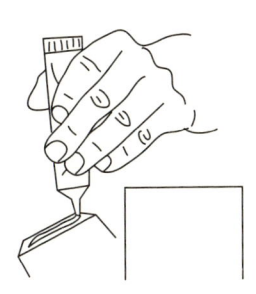

Fig. 3. **Carefully secure the edges with glue.**

Fig. 4. **Set the dog house on fire. Prepare for catharsis.**

THE INTERMENT

HEADSTONES

Many owners opt to make a wooden grave marker for their pet. This has the advantage of being simple and, when treated with preservative, will last for some time. A cross is easily made following the directions given here, and, if you're not experienced enough at whittling to carve the necessary lettering, you can paint or even stencil names, dates, and perhaps an appropriate quote without too much difficulty.

Alternatively, you could commission a professional stonemason for a really substantial headstone; this will be costly, though, so be sure to ask for detailed drawings before work commences. As the client, make sure that you are

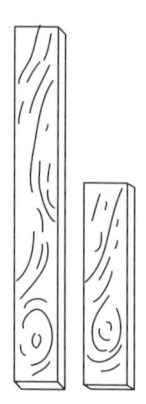

Fig. 1. The two pieces for your cross should be equal in weight, but the upright should be at least one and a half times the length of the crosspiece.

Fig. 2. Use sturdy twine or fine wire to bind the two pieces firmly together. Tuck the final twist or knot between the pieces for a neat finish.

HEADSTONES

completely happy with the design before the cutting and carving starts: Changing your mind about size, shape, or inscription when the mason is halfway through the commission will be awkward. Take time to decide exactly what you want in order to avoid later, potentially expensive, regret. Do some preliminary sketches and show them to your friends and family. Do not be afraid to seek advice or feedback. This is a once in a lifetime decision. If you want a memorial that's more solid than wood, but more economical than the full mason-designed option, you could choose a large, irregularly shaped stone or a small boulder and paint your lettering on it. This will give you an attractively rugged, hand-hewn effect at absolutely no outlay, and with the expenditure of only a very little effort.

> *Ye! who behold perchance*
> *this simple urn,*
> *Pass on, it honours none*
> *you wish to mourn.*
> *To mark a friend's remains*
> *these stones arise;*
> *I never knew but one—*
> *and here he lies.*
>
> Lord Byron, *"Epitaph to a Dog"*

Fig. 3. Remember that about a third of the length of the upright should be sunk into the ground to keep your cross securely upright.

THE INTERMENT

URNS AND MAUSOLEUMS

Fig. 1. **Memorial urns can be as simple or as elaborate as you wish.**

If you are not intending to bury or scatter the remains of your companion, you will need somewhere to keep him. A spice jar or even a tobacco tin is fine if your pet was a simple, homespun sort of character (though of course if you do use a tobacco tin, you should keep it out of the way, to avoid unseemly accidents). As we mentioned before, a stylish urn makes rather more of a statement, and urns are widely available. Some commercial examples are rather vulgar and lachrymose, so it's as well to wait until the initial throes of grief have subsided before making a purchase that you might later feel obliged to keep from public display on grounds of taste.

If you have an appropriate space, a mausoleum is a striking and unusual repository for the deceased. This is usually a brick or stone-built building, but unless you work in the construction industry this might be a bit much to ask. However, a miniature wooden Greek temple is quite easy to build, as shown here. Measure up the materials according to the size of the urn to be housed and the degree of

URNS AND MAUSOLEUMS

admiration that you wish to inspire. If it is to be situated outdoors, you should paint or varnish the temple to protect it from the elements. When it is complete you can place the cremation urn within it. More impressive still, you could put the remains in a plain box and have a sculpted effigy of the deceased made to sit on top. When placed inside the mausoleum, this catafalque will be a fitting resting place for a noble companion.

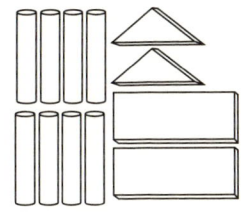

Fig. 2. Gather the different elements for the mausoleum before you start construction.

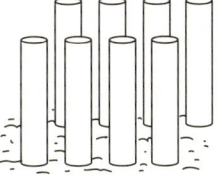

Fig. 3. Anchor the supporting pillars firmly in the ground.

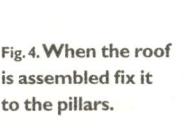

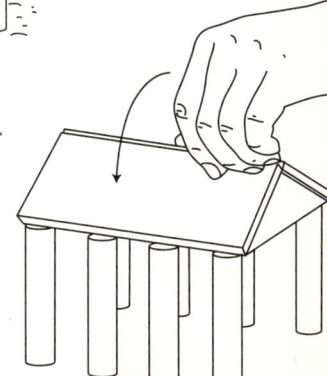

Fig. 4. When the roof is assembled fix it to the pillars.

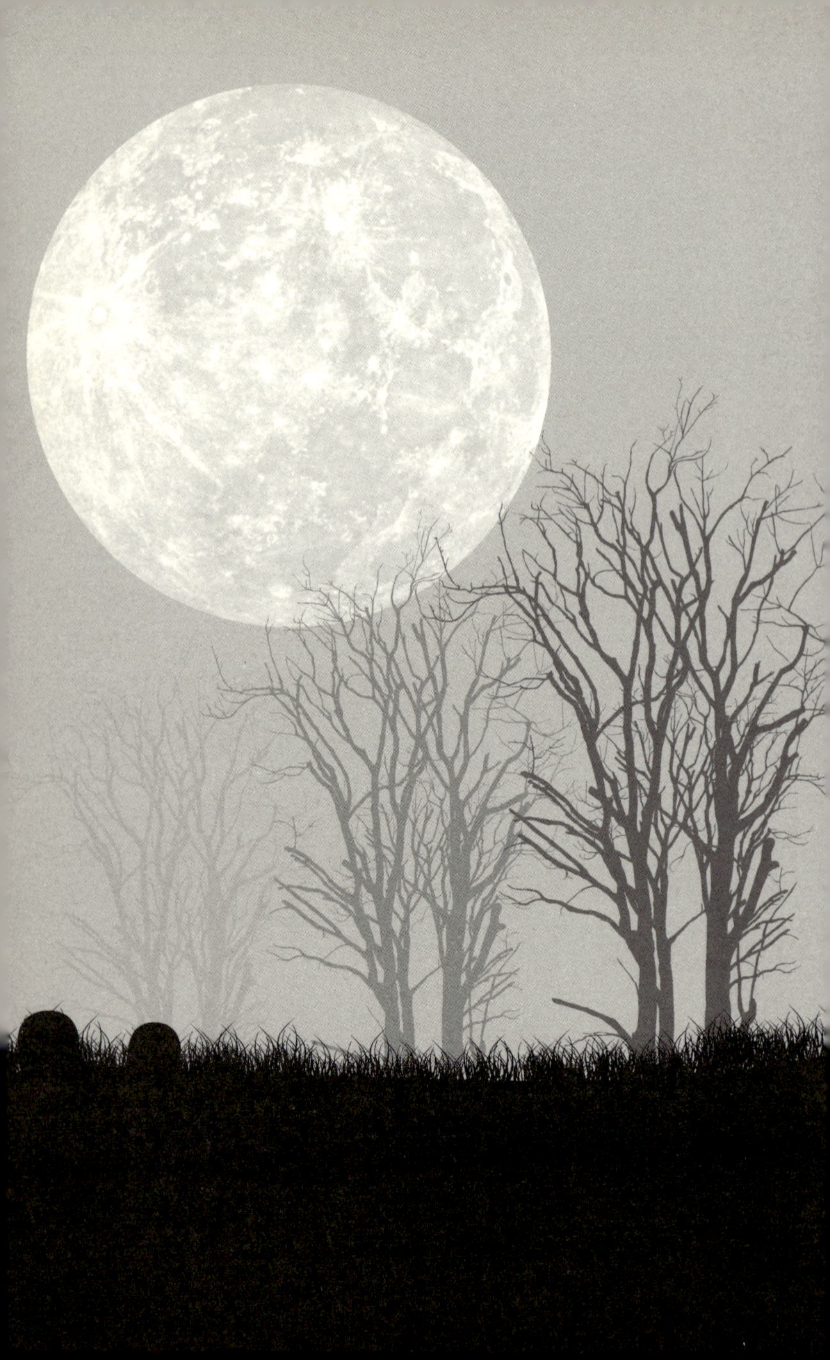

THE AFTERMATH

THE AFTERMATH

THE MOURNING PERIOD

Grieve in your own time, your own way, and indeed for as long as you feel necessary. Scheduling grief is not a realistic option, even for those with demanding careers and personal lives. Your neighbor may announce that he or she has reached closure after just a few days of mourning the departure of a dearly loved dog, but this does not require you to fast-forward your recovery from a cherished cat (you may find, however, that your children get over the loss of a gecko gone-to-its-maker more speedily than you are able to manage).

Fig. 1. Attending a pet-loss discussion group can bring unexpected solace and friendship. There is no need to grieve alone.

THE MOURNING PERIOD

Grief is not related to the size or longevity of the deceased. Like a chameleon, it can assume many hues. Time will mend the wound eventually, but in the interim you may go through various identifiable emotional stages, first of shock, then denial, and finally anger, before reaching acceptance and embarking on the deep-healing process.

Sharing your grief is to be advised in the denial stage. Join, or indeed initiate, a local pet-loss support group to share your memories and painful moments with others in the same situation. Take time to write a letter, poem, or song expressing your grief for your pet, and share it with the group. Helping others to overcome their loss will assist your own recovery. Write a journal, filling it with memories of happy times shared and relevant photographs. Keep some of your pet's possessions around the house: a much-used lead, a frayed cushion, a treasured, chewed toy, a framed skin shed by your snake. Creating a fully fledged shrine is, however, not recommended as this can lead to delays in the moving-on process.

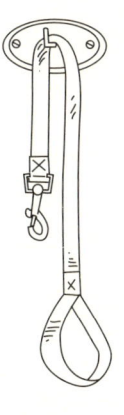

Fig. 2. A few key items belonging to the departed around the house can act like talismans.

Fig. 3. A journal can exorcize many grief demons.

THE AFTERMATH

MEMORIAL SERVICES

Fig. 1. Tasteful, themed refreshments are to be recommended at a memorial service.

Your relationship with your pet—although now brought to its allotted physical conclusion—will continue in spirit, and so it is natural to wish to commemorate and even celebrate it. A memorial service to mark your pet's birthday, or the first anniversary of his unfortunate demise, is both appropriate and to be encouraged.

Make the service a memorable occasion: An expression of gratitude, with the potential for delivering comfort and a degree of closure. If the opening event is a success, you might even want to institute an annual gathering. Although at its core lie loss and grief, a memorial service (no matter how short) can bring solace in recollection and joy in celebration. Welcome close friends, family, and pet sitters to gather together and say a few words that highlight your very personal relationship with your pet. Give thanks, separately and together. Invite descendants of the deceased—reuniting them for the event if they are homed elsewhere (and if distance, numbers, size, and facilities permit; twelve

MEMORIAL SERVICES

rottweilers, large and small, could potentially be troublesome in a small space)—for their very lives are a monument to the departed.

Pay tribute to your pet with a reading, either from a published work or by quoting extracts from your own journal (*see page 115*). Read a poem, and don't be afraid to read lines penned by your own children. Poignancy is not the preserve of the professionals.

Fig. 2. **Prayers, hymns, songs, music, candles, flowers, and photographs will add meaning and poignancy.**

SEANCES

Although widely discredited as the preserve of cranks, fraudsters, and the irredeemably credulous, the psychic realm does have its adherents. If you are keenly aware of the silence that has fallen since your pet passed over, or if you feel there were things you never got around to saying while he was alive, or if he hid your vehicle keys shortly before expiring and you have been unable to find them, there's no sense in letting the materialist objections of Enlightenment rationalism prevent you from making the effort to keep in touch.

Fig. 1. A spirit board is one way to get in touch with the deceased, though it does require them to be good at spelling.

Bear in mind that seances can be expensive—the spirit world being, as it is, difficult to contact—so it's a good idea to collect a group of like-minded owners of deceased pets and share the medium's fee. You should have the questions you want to ask written down, so as not to be caught out when the moment comes. And don't forget: If your pet didn't speak in life, it's unlikely (though not impossible) that he will do so after death. You may have to be satisfied with a few squeaks, squawks, or woofs, depending on the

SEANCES

species. Most reputable mediums are trained to interpret tapping or whistling sounds, however, and so will be able to offer responses to the questions you ask. And even if no audible response is elicited, you might well be able to sense, with the help of the medium, the general aura around your pet's spirit, which can be a comforting experience.

Fig. 2. **A gifted medium should be able to summon the aura of your former companion.**

THE AFTERMATH

INTERNET MEMORIALS

Fig. 1. An online memorial offers endless possibilities to the grieving but gifted webmaster.

The Internet is, of course, the greatest meeting place on Earth, teeming with ideas, thoughts, emotions, visions and people and accessible to practically everyone. Where better to establish a memorial to your former pet than where it can be seen and responded to on a global scale?

There are plenty of sources of free web space if all you want to do is set up a photo gallery with a brief biography of your pet and some reflections on your life together. If, however, you are a bit of a whiz with applets and Java and so on, you might want to register a domain name (www.inmemoryofrex.org, perhaps) and invest in sufficient MBs to set up something a little more spectacular.

You could incorporate some film of Pip in action, climbing trees, relishing a juicy carrot, retrieving mice, or giving birth to the umpteenth litter, as appropriate. You could add footage of the obsequies themselves, so that visitors could share in the parting ceremony. You could set up a blog to offer periodic updates on how you are getting through the process of Living Without Pip, and invite readers to post their own experiences of pet bereavement. Better still, you could offer other bereaved pet owners the opportunity to buy space on the site to set up their own memorials, and could become the center of a global family of mourners united in their search for solace in the face of mortality. In this way, the loss of Pip becomes a source of both comfort and hope for people he never met, in places he never visited—a fine memorial indeed.

> *The comfort of having a friend*
> *may be taken away,*
> *but not that of having had one.*
> Seneca

THE AFTERMATH

YOUR PET'S WORLDLY GOODS

Fig. 1. You might want to keep some of your pet's belongings as a constant reminder of him.

After the ceremonies have ended, the guests have all gone home, and the last few dog chews have been swept up from the floor of the reception room, you will be left with a petless house and one final task to perform: disposing of the deceased's personal effects.

The scale of the job will vary according to the species of the deceased and the length of time he was with you. Stick insects don't leave behind much evidence of their existence beyond their vivarium, while tortoises—for all their longevity—are similarly light travelers through this vale of tears. Dogs and cats are

YOUR PET'S WORDLY GOODS

liable to have accumulated all manner of material goods, and these will now quite possibly be too painful a reminder of what has gone before.

Of course, you might have followed the ancient habit of sending your pet into the afterlife with all the ID tags, scratching boards, squeaky toys, and tennis balls that he will need to enjoy to the fullest the great beyond. Burying everything with the deceased or consigning the belongings to the pyre with their former owner is a neat and decisive way out of the dilemma. However, if this seems too callous or too wasteful for your liking, gather everything together and take the things to your local charity store, or put them in a basket in your front yard with a notice reading: "Free to pets with not enough toys." You'll feel a warm glow on seeing a lively dog or curious cat picking out a fresh plaything.

Fig. 2. **Distributing your pet's toys to other pets can be a difficult but rewarding gesture.**

> *All of the animals except for man know that the principal business of life is to enjoy it.*
> Samuel Butler

MOVING ON

Fig. 1. You cannot schedule or plan grief. Give yourself plenty of time to recover from your loss.

The grief process, like its length, is very personal. The timing of your readiness to take on another companion will be equally idiosyncratic. Your relationship was rich, rewarding, and rare, and—like your pet itself—not interchangeable or easily replaced. Allow yourself time to grieve. Don't be tempted to fill the void with a new pet simply because there is a dog- or cat-shaped hole in your life. New pets must be appreciated for their own sake, for the contribution they can make to your future, rather than for their ability to mask the pain of the past.

Wait until you feel—indeed, you know—the time is right. What are the signs? When you come to terms with the sense of loss and sadness in your life and can convert it into thoughts of happy companionship to come; when talk of your pet makes you laugh and smile without feelings of guilt or a sense of betrayal; when you turn the pages of the calendar forward, not back. Remember, moving on does not mean that you have forgotten. It is simply an acknowledgment that you have reached a place in which you are finally able

MOVING ON

to integrate the pain of past loss with healing hope for the future. Moving on is exactly that: You are ready to make emotional, even physical, progress, to look at the new pages in the diary or calendar and not at the old ones. Keep a special place in your home and heart for your old friend, but create a new and exciting space alongside to be filled by a companion full of fresh life and potential.

Fig. 2. **Keep a memento of your pet. He is gone but not forgotten.**

You may want to consider a different breed or, indeed, different species. Follow your instinct. Move the ball down the field. You will be bruised and sadder, but wiser. That's life.

Fig. 3. **You will know when the time is right to think about introducing a new pet into your home.**

GLOSSARY

ashes: the remains of the deceased after cremation; strictly speaking, these are not ashes at all, but fragments of bone, and are often more accurately referred to as "cremains".

bereavement: deprivation of a loved one by death.

catacomb: an underground tomb, often cut out of the rock.

catafalque: a decorated structure used to support a coffin during a period of lying-in.

cyrogenic preservation: method of keeping an animal in suspended animation pending a miracle of science that will cure whatever it is suffering from.

embalming: the process of protecting a dead body against decay by removing the organs and injecting preservative fluid.

epitaph: a few kind words about the deceased, usually inscribed on a headstone, *see* eulogy.

eulogy: a few kind words on the deceased, usually spoken at the funeral ceremony, *see* epitaph.

hereafter: pet heaven.

interment: the consigning of the deceased to the earth.

lying-in: a period during which the deceased remains on display for friends and relatives to say their last farewells.

mausoleum: an often ornate or splendid edifice for housing the remains of the deceased.

mourning period: the period of time after a bereavement before you are respectably allowed to start enjoying yourself again.

obsequies: grandiose term for funeral rites.

pyre: a cremation bonfire, usually held in the open air and often of extravagant proportions.

rigor mortis: stiffening of the body after death.

vigil: attendance upon the deceased the night before the funeral, usually performed by close relatives.

wake: like a vigil, but is often more boisterous.

FURTHER READING

Moira Anderson *Coping with Sorrow on the Loss of Your Pet*

David Congalton *Three Cats, Two Dogs: One Journey Through Multiple Pet Loss*

Lorri A. Greene and **Jacquelyn Landis** *Saying Good-Bye to the Pet You Love: A Complete Resource to Help You Heal*

Robin Grey *Coping with Pet Loss*

Chuck Iglesias *Get Stuffed—The Home Taxidermist's Handbook*

Gary Kurz *Cold Noses at the Pearly Gates*

Jane Matthews *Losing a Pet: Coping with the Death of Your Beloved Animal*

Rita M. Reynolds *Blessing the Bridge: What Animals Teach Us about Death and Dying*

Kim Sheridan *Animals and the Afterlife: True Stories of Our Best Friends' Journey Beyond Death*

Scott S. Smith *The Soul of Your Pet: Evidence for the Survival of Animals After Death*

Emily Margaret Stuparyk *When Only the Love Remains: The Pain of Pet Loss*

USEFUL WEB SITES

www.aplb.org
The Association for Pet Loss and Bereavement: an association of members who are experienced and knowledgeable in the area of pet death and its effects on those who mourn this loss

www.heavenlystarsfireworks.com
Bury the deceased in space

www.iaopc.com
International Association of Pet Cemeteries and Crematories

www.ILovedMyPet.com
www.imorialpets.com
Two pet memorial sites

www.petloss.com
The Pet Loss Grief Support Web site: A gentle and compassionate Web site for pet lovers who are grieving over the death of a pet or an ill pet

INDEX

agar jelly 57

borax 35
breaking the news 26–7
bronzing 47

charitable donations 77, 123
children 26–7, 52, 53, 57, 77, 81, 82, 83, 114, 117
chloroform 19
cloning 14–15
coffins 40–3
　cats 60–3
　dogs 64–7
　finishing and lining 50, 52, 54, 59, 67, 68–71
　fish 56–9
　insects 44–7
　ornamentation 42–3, 45, 54, 55, 61, 67, 71
　reptiles 48–51
　rodents and rabbits 52–5
　sea burial 102–3
　tennis-ball coffin 52, 53
confirming death 24–5
cremation 24, 64, 65, 87, 100–1, 102, 105
　urns/mausoleums 64, 110–11
cryogenic preservation 15, 32–3

decomposition 30

eco-friendly disposal 36–7, 41, 43, 51, 55, 63
embalming 29, 30–1, 74
eulogies 84
euthanasia 18–19
excarnation 36–7, 104–5

film 31, 121
floral tributes 76–7
food 44, 77, 94–5, 116
formaldehyde 30
freezer 29, 30, 55, 58
funeral procession 80–1
funerals 12, 33, 43, 74–95

gilding 47
grave, location 16–17, 21, 78, 98–9
grave goods 106–7
grieving process 20, 61, 114–15, 124

headstones 108–9
hearses 76, 78–9
humanist funerals 88–9

insurance 12–13
Internet memorials 120–1

journal 106, 115

Latin tags or mottos 71
lying-in 30, 41, 48, 57, 74

mausoleums 110–11
memorial services 116–17
mourning period 29, 114–15, 124
moving on 124–5
music 74, 81, 82, 83, 87, 90, 91

Native American culture 36, 104
new pets 124, 125

order of service 82–3

pagan rites 86–7
personal effects 122–3
personality 12, 40, 42, 77, 88, 90, 110
photographs 10, 11, 59, 93, 106, 117, 120
poetry 75, 84, 85, 102, 115, 117
portraits 10, 59
preservation 28–35, 65

readings 75, 84-5, 102, 117
reception 94–5
refrigerator 29, 57
remembrance book 93
rigor mortis 25, 28, 48, 60

sea burial 102–3
seances 118–19
shock 20, 115
shrines 11, 115
skeleton 36, 37
skinning 35
sky burial 104–5
sudden death 20–1
support group 114, 115

T-shirts 11, 93
taxidermy 34–5
Tibetan Buddhist culture 36, 104

urns 64, 110–11

veterinarians 10, 18, 19, 21, 24, 100
vigils 74–5
Viking funeral 103

wakes 74–5
wreaths 76–7